SECOND EDITION

CW01401396

Life

STUDENT'S BOOK | INTERMEDIATE

NATIONAL GEOGRAPHIC
LEARNING

HELEN STEPHENSON
PAUL DUMMETT
JOHN HUGHES

Australia · Brazil · Mexico · Singapore · United Kingdom · United States

Contents Split Edition A

Unit	Grammar	Vocabulary	Real life (functions)	Pronunciation
1 Culture and identity	present simple and present continuous stative verbs question forms: direct questions question forms: indirect questions	word focus: *love* feelings wordbuilding: adjective and noun collocations	opening and closing conversations	direct questions short questions
VIDEO: Faces of India ▶ REVIEW				
2 Performing	present perfect simple *already*, *just* and *yet* present perfect simple and past simple	musical styles emotions word focus: *kind* describing performances	choosing an event	weak forms intonation with *really, absolutely,* etc.
VIDEO: Taiko master ▶ REVIEW				
3 Water	past simple and past continuous past perfect	describing experiences wordbuilding: adverbs word focus: *get*	telling stories	*d* and *t* after *-ed* endings *was* and *were*
VIDEO: Four women and a wild river ▶ REVIEW				
4 Opportunities	predictions future forms	word focus: *job* and *work* education wordbuilding: prefix *re-* pay and conditions job requirements	making and responding to requests	weak and strong auxiliary verbs
VIDEO: Everest tourism changed Sherpa lives ▶ REVIEW				
5 Wellbeing	modal verbs first conditional: *if + will* when, as soon as, unless, until, before	a healthy lifestyle word focus: *so* restaurants	describing dishes	weak forms disappearing sounds
VIDEO: Dangerous dining ▶ REVIEW				
6 Mysteries	purpose: *to ... , for ...* and *so that ...* certainty and possibility	word focus: *long* art wordbuilding: nouns and verbs *-ly* adverbs in stories	reacting to surprising news	weak form of *have* showing interest and disbelief
VIDEO: Encounters with a sea monster ▶ REVIEW				

Listening	Reading	Critical thinking	Speaking	Writing
an extract from a TV programme about Native American culture two people doing a quiz about colours and their meaning	an article about cultural identity an article about globalization	examples	getting to know you my language course how international you feel first impressions	text type: a business profile writing skill: criteria for writing
three people talking about arts events a man talking about his dance academy	an article about listening to music an article about performance art	balance	new releases performing a survey on the arts arts events	text type: a review writing skill: linking ideas (1)
an extract from a radio programme about recreation in the water interviews about what happened next	an interview about underwater discoveries an article about an unforgettable experience	drawing conclusions	the first time what had happened learning a lesson it happened to me	text type: a blog post writing skill: interesting language
three people talking about their childhood ambitions three women talking about decisions	an article about the future of work an article about the economic boom in China	the author's view	predictions planning your work the perfect job requests	text type: a covering letter writing skill: formal style
an extract from a radio programme about healthy eating two people discussing the power of the mind	a news item about traditional dishes a news item about imaginary eating an article about modern lifestyles	writer's purpose	rules and regulations consequences modern life restaurant dishes	text type: a formal letter/email writing skill: explaining consequences
two people discussing an unusual photo a speaker at a conference talking about a mystery an extract from a radio programme about the Nasca lines	an article about flexible thinking an article about one of aviation's greatest mysteries	speculation or fact?	what's it for? speculating comparing ideas surprising news	text type: a news story writing skill: structuring a news story

Contents Split Edition B

Unit	Grammar	Vocabulary	Real life (functions)	Pronunciation
7 Living space pages 9–20	*used to*, *would* and past simple comparison: adverbs comparison: patterns	in the city wordbuilding: noun → adjective word focus: *as* and *like*	stating preferences and giving reasons	rising and falling intonation
VIDEO: The town with no wi-fi **page 18** ▶ REVIEW **page 20**				
8 Travel pages 21–32	verb patterns: *-ing* form and *to* + infinitive present perfect simple and continuous How long?	holiday activities travel problems wordbuilding: compound nouns	dealing with problems	strong and weak forms
VIDEO: Questions and answers **page 30** ▶ REVIEW **page 32**				
9 Shopping pages 33–44	passives articles and quantifiers	shopping (1) wordbuilding: compound adjectives shopping (2)	buying things	linking silent letters
VIDEO: Making a deal **page 42** ▶ REVIEW **page 44**				
10 No limits pages 45–56	second conditional defining relative clauses	medicine word focus: *take* injuries	talking about injuries	sentence stress *and*
VIDEO: What does an astronaut dream about? **page 54** ▶ REVIEW **page 56**				
11 Connections pages 57–68	reported speech reporting verbs	communications technology	telephone language	contrastive stress polite requests with *can* and *could*
VIDEO: Can you read my lips? **page 66** ▶ REVIEW **page 68**				
12 Experts pages 69–80	third conditional *should have* and *could have*	wordbuilding: prefixes *in-*, *un-*, *im-* word focus: *go*	making and accepting apologies	*should have* and *could have* sentence stress
VIDEO: Shark vs. octopus **page 78** ▶ REVIEW **page 80**				

COMMUNICATION ACTIVITIES **page 81** ▶ GRAMMAR SUMMARY **page 83** ▶ AUDIOSCRIPTS **page 97**

Listening	Reading	Critical thinking	Speaking	Writing
three people talking about different living arrangements podcast replies about house design	an article about what New York used to be like an article about a little town in Puerto Rico	descriptions	places advice a tourist destination choices	text type: a description of a place writing skill: organizing ideas
three people talking about travel tips people talking about their holidays an extract from a radio programme about a wildlife conservationist	an article about writers returning to their roots an article about tourism	close reading	holiday companions favourite activities going green travel problems	text type: a text message writing skill: informal style
market research interviews with three people who are shopping an extract from a radio programme about impulse buying	an article about two ways of going shopping an article about how to negotiate a price	testing a conclusion	shopping now and in the future my things souvenirs buying things	text type: customer feedback writing skill: clarity: pronouns
a podcast about the *Marathon des Sables* an extract from a TV preview show about bionic bodies	an article about life on another planet two stories about acts of endurance	reading between the lines	I'd love to live in … medicine inspirational people talking about injuries	text type: a personal email writing skill: linking ideas (2)
four conversations about the news four conversations about news headlines	an article about isolated tribes an article about community journalism	opinions	news stories personal communication apps for mobile phones telephone messages	text type: an opinion essay writing skill: essay structure
an interview with a farmer two stories about unexpected problems	a review of a book about Arctic expeditions an article about the samurai	relevance	decisions where did I go wrong? going back in time making and accepting apologies	text type: a website article writing skill: checking your writing

Life around the world – in 12 videos

Unit 6 Encounters with a sea monster

Three people tell their stories about what they saw in the water.

Unit 12 Shark vs. octopus

What happens when a shark and an octopus meet.

Unit 2 Taiko master

The history of Taiko drumming from its origins in Japan to modern-day San Francisco.

Canada

USA

UK

Spain

Morocco

Unit 7 The town with no wi-fi

Find out what life is like in the quiet zone of Green Bank.

Unit 11 Can you read my lips?

Rachel Kolb tells us about communicating as a deaf person.

Peru

Unit 8 Questions and answers

National Geographic Explorers from Spain, the UK, Peru and other countries talk about their roles and about objects that are important to them in their work.

Unit 10 What does an astronaut dream about?

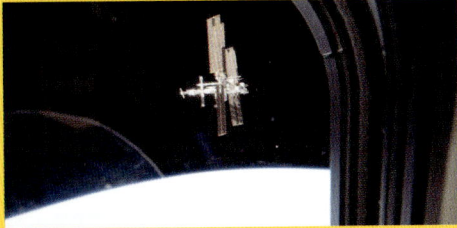

British astronaut Helen Sharman describes her experience of being on the Mir space station.

Unit 3 Four women and a wild river

Amber Valenti leads a kayak trip down the Amur River in Mongolia, Russia and China.

Russia

Unit 9 Making a deal

Learn how to bargain in Morocco.

Mongolia

Japan

China

Nepal

Unit 5 Dangerous dining

Find out why people eat the most dangerous fish on Earth – fugu.

India

Unit 1 Faces of India

Find out about Rajasthan through a focus on its people and faces.

Unit 4 Everest tourism changed Sherpa lives

Find out if Everest tourism has been a good or a bad thing for the local people.

Split Editions A and B

UNIT 1 CULTURE AND IDENTITY

UNIT 2 PERFORMING

UNIT 3 WATER

UNIT 4 OPPORTUNITIES

UNIT 5 WELLBEING

UNIT 6 MYSTERIES

UNIT 7 LIVING SPACE

UNIT 8 TRAVEL

UNIT 9 SHOPPING

UNIT 10 NO LIMITS

UNIT 11 CONNECTIONS

UNIT 12 EXPERTS

Unit 7 Living space

Off the Izu peninsula, Honshu, Japan, a yellow goby looks at the camera.

FEATURES

10 Before New York

What came before the city?

12 Homes around the world

An architect talks about homes

14 Sweet songs and strong coffee

Visit a community in Puerto Rico

18 The town with no wi-fi

A video about an unusual town

1 Work in pairs. Look at the photo. Discuss the questions.

1 What can you see in the photo?
2 Where do you think this photo was taken?
3 Do you think this is the fish's natural habitat, a temporary shelter or a permanent home?

2 ▶ 54 Listen to three people talking about different living arrangements. Write the number of the speaker (1–3) next to the statements that summarize their comments.

a I can't wait to leave my parents' house and get some independence.
b My family's lovely, but I'd like to have my own home and some privacy.
c My flatmates aren't here much, so it's just like having my own place really.
d It's cramped and noisy, but at least you're never lonely.
e Sharing a flat with friends is not as easy as I thought it would be.
f I love living with my mum and dad and brothers. I won't leave until I get married.

3 Work in groups. Discuss the questions.

1 Which room do you spend most time in at home?
2 How do different family members use different rooms?
3 Do you consider your home a private place, just for family? Or do you often have friends round?

7a Before New York

Vocabulary in the city

1 Work in pairs. What kind of a place is New York? Try to describe New York in three words.

2 Complete the sentences with these words. Which sentences do you think are true of New York?

> atmosphere   blocks   built-up   financial   neighbourhoods
> public transport   residents   skyscrapers

1 There's an excellent _____ system to get you around the city.
2 It's got an important business and _____ district.
3 It's one of the most _____ places you can live, with few open spaces.
4 The views from the _____ are spectacular, especially at night.
5 There's lots to do, both for tourists and _____ .
6 Some _____ are more dangerous than others.
7 The _____ is exciting and lively.
8 The streets divide the city into _____ .

3 Write sentences about places you know with the words from Exercise 2.

Reading

4 Work in pairs. Discuss the questions. Then read the article *Before New York* and check your ideas.

1 What do you think the area that is now New York was like before the city was built?
2 What kind of people do you think lived there?
3 What kind of landscapes do you think there were?

5 Read the article again. Answer the questions in your own words.

1 What's the connection between Eric Sanderson and the image with the article?
2 What did Sanderson aim to do with his project?
3 Why do you think the appearance of the beaver in 2007 was important for Sanderson?

Before New York

By Peter Miller

▶ 55

Of all the visitors to New York City in recent years, one of the most surprising was a beaver which appeared one morning in 2007. Although beavers used to be common in the area in the seventeenth century, and people used to hunt them for their skins, there haven't been any for more than two hundred years.

For ecologist Eric Sanderson, the beaver's appearance was especially interesting. For ten years, Sanderson has been in charge of a project to show what the area used to look like before the city changed it completely. As Sanderson says, 'There are views in this city where you cannot see, except for a person, another living thing. Not a tree or a plant. How did a place become like that?'

In fact, long before the skyscrapers came to dominate the view, this place was a pristine wilderness where animals like beavers, bears and turkeys would move freely through forests, marshes and grassland. There used to be sandy beaches along the coasts and ninety kilometres of fresh-water streams.

At the end of Sanderson's project, he built a 3D computer model of the area. (See the top photo on the right.) You can pick any spot in modern New York and see what used to be there. Take Fifth Avenue, for example. A family called Murray used to have a farm here and in 1782 (during the American War of Independence) the British soldiers landed near here. 'I'd like every New Yorker to know that they live in a place with amazing natural potential – even if you have to look a little harder to see it,' says Sanderson.

> pristine (adj) /ˈprɪstiːn/ pure, as new
> wilderness (n) /ˈwɪldənəs/ an area in a completely natural state

Grammar *used to*, *would* and past simple

> ▶ **USED TO**
>
> 1 People **used to hunt** beavers for their skins.
> 2 The Murray family **used to have** a farm here.
> 3 There **didn't use to be** any skyscrapers.
> 4 What **did** New York **use to look** like?
>
> ▶ **WOULD**
>
> Beavers, bears and turkeys **would move** freely.
>
> For further information and practice, see page 84.

6 Look at the grammar box and the article. Underline the sentences in the article with *used to* and *would*. Do they refer to past habits and states or to single actions in the past?

7 Look at the article again. Find three examples of single actions in the past. What is the verb form?

8 Look at the grammar box. Match the sentences with *used to* (1–4) with the uses (a or b). Then match the sentence with *would* with its use.

  a   past state
  b   past habit (repeated action)

Computer Generated Image (top) by Markley Boyer

9 Rewrite the sentences using *used to* + infinitive where possible.

  1   New York was a lot greener than it is now.
  2   The early residents didn't live in a large city.
  3   People farmed the land.
  4   Farmers hunted wild animals for food.
  5   Soldiers fought an important battle on the island.
  6   What was in the area where Fifth Avenue is now?

10 Complete the text with the past simple, *used to* or *would* form of the verbs. In some cases, you can use more than one form.

> I remember when I first ¹ .... (move) to New York from California with my parents. Every day for the first month, I ² .... (stand) in the street and stare up at the skyscrapers. They ³ .... (be) taller than anything I'd ever seen. The streets ⁴ .... (be) much busier than in California and I ⁵ .... (run) from one side to the other holding my mother's hand. For the first few months, we ⁶ .... (not / go) further than four blocks from home. My parents ⁷ .... (not / own) a car, so on Sunday mornings we ⁸ .... (take) the subway to Central Park. We ⁹ .... (have) breakfast at a lovely deli and then we ¹⁰ .... (go) skating. The city ¹¹ .... (be) a lot more dangerous and scary then.

11 Complete the sentences with the past simple, *used to* or *would* so that they are true for you. Then work in pairs. Compare your sentences and ask follow-up questions about three of the sentences.

  1   Before I worked / studied here, I … .
  2   When I was in primary school, I … .
  3   Before we moved here, my family … .
  4   I remember my first holiday. I … .
  5   Whenever I had exams at school, I … .
  6   In my family, at weekends we … .
  7   The first time I went to school alone, … .
  8   As a child, I … .

Speaking 〈 my life 〉

12 Choose two places from the list. How have the places changed? Make notes for then and now.

  • my street   • my school
  • my home   • my village / my town
  • my classroom

  my street: then – lots of cars; now – residents only

13 Work in pairs. Tell each other about the places you chose in Exercise 12. Use *used to* and *would*. Decide which places have changed the most and whether they are better now than they were in the past.

  A: *There **used to be** a lot of cars in my street, but now only residents can park on it.*
  B: *What do visitors do? Can they drive up to your house?*

7b Homes around the world

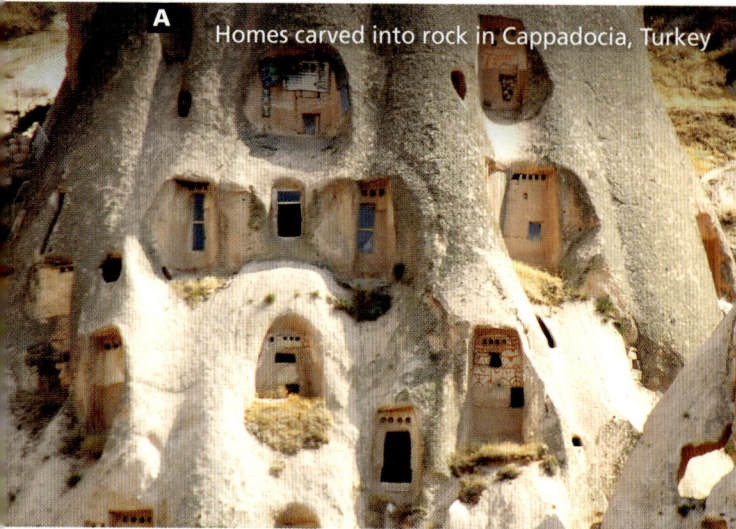

A Homes carved into rock in Cappadocia, Turkey

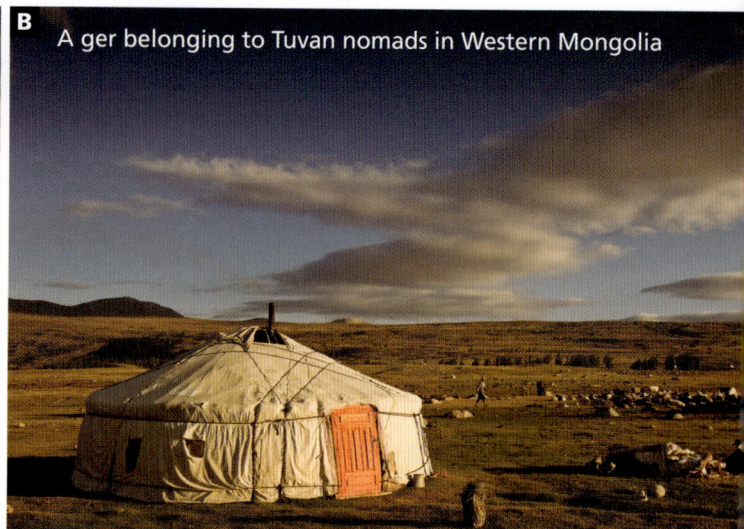

B A ger belonging to Tuvan nomads in Western Mongolia

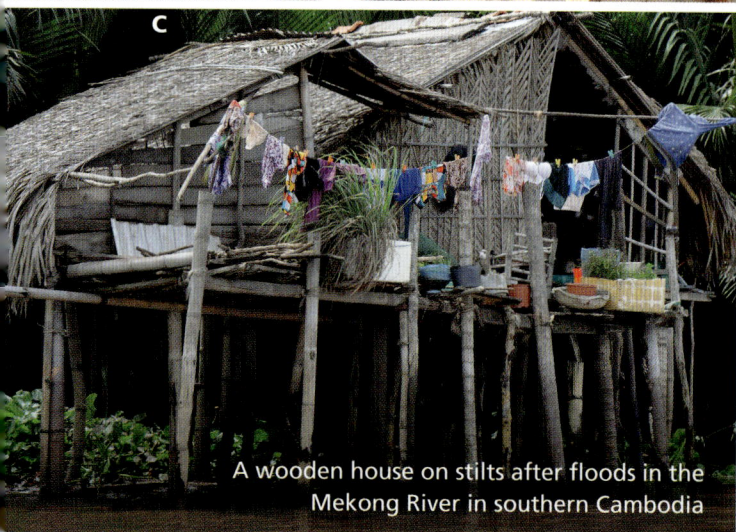

C A wooden house on stilts after floods in the Mekong River in southern Cambodia

D Modern terraced houses in Sabah, Borneo

Listening

1 Look at the photos of four homes. What are they made of?

> bricks   cloth   rock   wood

2 Think of a question you'd like to ask each home owner. Then work in pairs. Tell your partner.

3 ▶ 56 Marta Fereira presents the TV series *Home Planet*. Read the questions (a–e) that viewers have sent in to the programme's website. Then listen and match Marta's podcast replies (1–5) with the questions.

a   Why are you so interested in traditional house design?   *1*
b   We live in a new house that my dad calls a 'box'. What do you think of the design of modern houses?
c   Why are some types of house more common in some areas of the world than in others?
d   You mentioned shelters in your last programme. What's the difference between a shelter and a home?
e   I'd like to stay in a ger, but they look a bit basic. What are they really like?

4 ▶ 56 Listen again and complete the sentences.

1   Traditional houses usually survive bad .... conditions better than modern ones.
2   Rock homes heat up less quickly than ....
3   You can put up a ger much faster than a ....
4   You can live much more safely above the ....
5   Modern houses are getting smaller and ....
6   Unfortunately, sometimes .... are also built badly.
7   Modern houses don't work as efficiently as ....

5 Which of the homes in the photos would you like to spend time in? Why?

Grammar comparison: adverbs

▶ **COMPARATIVE ADVERBS**

Adverb *quickly/easily*	Comparative forms **more** *quickly/easily* **(than)** **less** *quickly/easily* **(than)** **not as** *quickly/easily* **as** **as** *quickly/easily* **as**

Note: *well* → *better, badly* → *worse, fast* → *faster*

For further information and practice, see page 84.

6 Look at the grammar box. Underline the comparative adverbs in the sentences in Exercise 4.

7 Read the three sentences. Do they mean the same thing? Do you agree with the sentences?

1 A brick house heats up more quickly than a rock house.
2 A rock house heats up less quickly than a brick house.
3 A rock house doesn't heat up as quickly as a brick house.

8 Complete the text about house sales and rentals in the UK with the comparative form of the adverbs.

Home	Properties	About	Contact	

Last year, terraced houses sold ¹ _____ (quickly) than flats, but one-bedroom flats did ² _____ (well) with young buyers. The number of large houses for rent rose ³ _____ (fast) than other types of home. Sales of large flats did ⁴ _____ (badly) than in previous years. So what does this mean for you? You can now rent a large house ⁵ _____ (cheaply) than ever before, but if you're trying to sell yours, you probably won't find a buyer ⁶ _____ (easily) as in previous years. Renting it out is a good alternative, so come and talk to us today.

9 Write sentences comparing the pairs of things. Then look at your partner's sentences. Do you agree?

1 young people / older people (drive carefully)
   Older people drive more carefully than young people.
2 girls / boys (do well in exams)
3 children / adults (learn quickly)
4 women / men (work hard)
5 Americans / British people (speak slowly)
6 I / my friends (sing badly)

Grammar comparison: patterns

▶ **COMPARATIVE PATTERNS**

*Modern houses are getting **smaller and smaller.**
House prices are going up **more and more quickly.**
And **the higher the stilts, the safer you are**.*

For further information and practice, see page 84.

10 Look at the grammar box. Which sentences describe change? Which sentence describes two related things?

11 Read what two people say about where they live. Underline comparative patterns similar to the ones in the grammar box.

Josef: As this building gets older, things go wrong more and more often. But living in a block of flats is really good because I don't have to worry about repairs and things. Everyone pays an amount each month, so the greater the number of residents, the lower the monthly payment is.

Sandra: We're all students. So for us, the cheaper the place, the better. We don't have as much money as people who are working. Rents are getting higher and higher, but you can still rent more cheaply than buy.

12 Complete what two more people say. Use comparative patterns.

Marcus: Neighbours! The ¹ _____ (few / good), I say. In my old flat, I used to have noisy people living right above me and I got ² _____ (angry) as the months went by. So I moved into my own house and life is much quieter now.

Frances: I love having a garden, but it's a lot of work – so the ³ _____ (small / good), I think. As time passes, the garden gets untidy ⁴ _____ (quickly), until in the end I have to do something about it.

Speaking my life

13 Work in groups of four. Discuss ways of doing these things. What advice would you give someone who wanted to do each one?

1 learn English more quickly
2 do better in exams
3 live more cheaply
4 eat more healthily
5 spend more wisely
6 shop more sensibly

A: *I think you can **learn English more quickly** if you go to live in an English-speaking country.*
B: *I agree. You won't learn **as quickly** if you stay at home. You won't meet native English speakers **as easily**, for example.*

7c Sweet songs and strong coffee

Reading

1 Think of one word to describe your home town. Tell the class.

2 Read the article about a town in Puerto Rico. What is the article mainly about? Choose the correct option (a–c).

  a daily life and work
  b festivals and holidays
  c people and traditions

3 Which paragraph gives information about:

  a what life used to be like in Adjuntas?
  b a traditional activity that people still do?
  c a new activity that people have learned to do?
  d what the town looks like?

4 Work in pairs. What can you remember about these things in Adjuntas?

  1 the horses   3 Lala Echevarria
  2 the town square   4 Tato Ramos

5 What do you think of Adjuntas as a place to live? Or a place to go on holiday? Tell your partner and give reasons using information from the article.

Wordbuilding noun → adjective

> ▶ **WORDBUILDING noun → adjective**
>
> We can make adjectives from nouns by adding a suffix such as -al or -ic. Spelling changes are sometimes needed.
> nature → natural, person → personal, artist → artistic
>
> For further practice, see Workbook page 59.

6 Look at the wordbuilding box. Find the adjectives in the article that are formed from these nouns.

  1 romance (line 10)   2 nation (line 16)

7 Complete the sentences with adjectives formed by adding -al or -ic to seven of the nouns.

benefit	centre	coast	economy	energy
fact	history	nature	origin	person

  1 The farmer never stops working. He's _____ and enthusiastic.
  2 The _____ part of the island is quite flat and the _____ part is mountainous.
  3 Opening the forest park was _____ for the villagers and the wildlife.
  4 We saw lots of birds in their _____ habitat.
  5 The _____ crisis hasn't affected business.
  6 The _____ area of the city around the old market is worth visiting.

Critical thinking descriptions

8 The writer aims to 'paint' a picture of Adjuntas in the reader's mind. Which descriptions in the article helped you to build a mental picture of Adjuntas? Underline words and phrases in the article.

9 Work in pairs. Compare the words you have underlined with your partner. Do you think the writer has been successful in her aims?

10 Add descriptions to each sentence to help the reader build a mental image. Then exchange sentences with your partner.

  1 The village is in the forest.
     The tiny village is in the heart of the dense forest.
  2 The houses are small.
  3 You can walk through the streets.
  4 The village centre is full of people.
  5 People are working everywhere you look.
  6 From one building, you can hear music.

Speaking ⟨ my life ⟩

11 Work in pairs. Choose a place that you both know well and that is attractive to tourists. Plan and practise a short presentation to persuade people to visit the destination. Use descriptions that help people to imagine the place. Talk about:

  • the best things to see
  • the best things to do
  • the best places to eat

12 Work in small groups. Give your presentation. Ask and answer follow-up questions.

  A: … and finally, don't leave the area without trying the food at the Golden Lion. It's delicious and not expensive.
  B: Can you tell me what kind of restaurant the Golden Lion is?

SWEET SONGS AND STRONG COFFEE

By Linda Gómez

▶ 57

There's a dreamy atmosphere to Adjuntas, a coffee town in the Valley of the Sleeping Giant high in the mountains of Puerto Rico. And there's love, the love of the people for their land and
5 its customs. People here say their families have lived here 'since forever'. You feel this love in the streets, with the smell of food cooked at roadside barbecues. You see it in the beautiful horses that parade through town on holidays. And you feel it as you sit in the
10 large, elegant square, with its romantic fountains and stone benches.

Several decades ago, this love of the land also led the local people to prevent a mining development in the surrounding mountains. They used money from
15 the area's successful coffee production to provide the money for a national park, El Bosque del Pueblo. The park opened in 1998 and runs a reforestation programme allowing young and old to plant trees. 'Learning to manage the forest has been a kind of
20 new life for us,' said Tinti Deya, a local resident. 'It's another world where we're like children doing everything for the first time, except in our case we're grandmothers.'

Grandmothers are everywhere in Adjuntas and
25 they're all respectfully addressed as Dofia. Lala Echevarria, an 85-year-old great-great-grandmother, was born on the oldest street in town, where she still lives in a small, neat and tidy home. Dofia Lala grew up before electricity and running water, and
30 remembers when the first car arrived in Adjuntas. 'As a child, I used to spend all my time carrying water, finding firewood, looking after the chickens and the cows,' she said. 'There were sixteen of us. We would wash our clothes in the river and we used to cook on
35 an open fire. At meal times, we kids would sit on the floor to eat.' Dofia Lala was working as a maid when she met and married the love of her life, Mariano the mechanic. They had thirteen children and shared 44 years before he died in 1983. She shows me the
40 dozens of photographs of four generations of her family that now fill her tiny home.

People in Adjuntas play old traditional songs in little shops like Lauro Yepez's place, where men meet to swap stories and have a drink. When I was there,
45 Tato Ramos, a local singer, appeared and began to sing in a flamenco style that hasn't changed for centuries. The shop quickly filled with working-class men clapping, tapping and nodding to the music. Ramos improvised songs on topics requested by
50 shop customers. 'This is a forgotten art,' said Yepez. 'People give him a topic and he composes a song, in proper rhyme.'

Later, I played the recording I'd made for my 88-year-old Spanish father, who has Alzheimer's disease. His
55 dark brown eyes shone with recognition. He nodded his head, smiled, and said, 'Oh yes, this I remember, this I remember …'

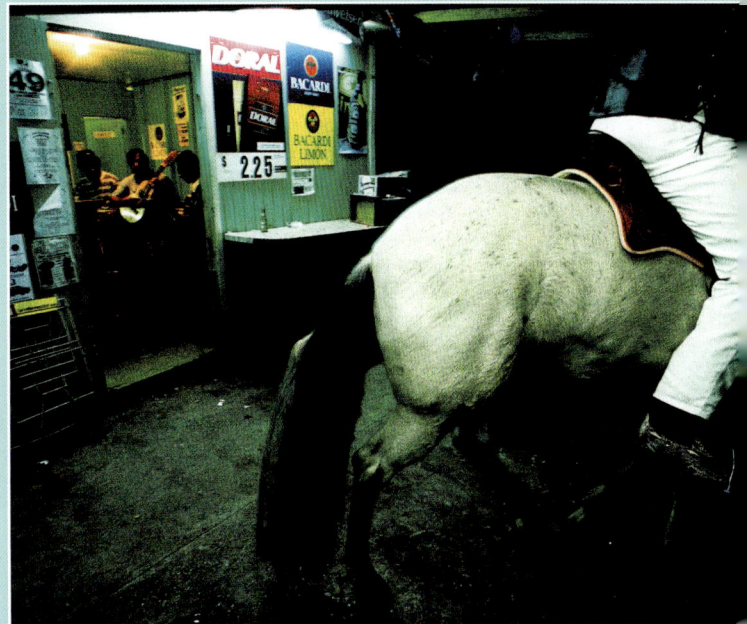

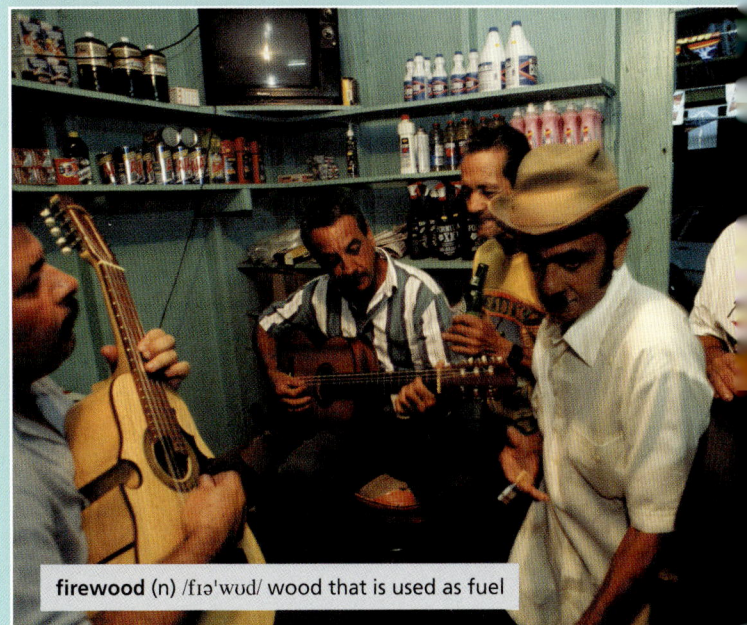

firewood (n) /ˈfɪəˌwʊd/ wood that is used as fuel

my life ▶ PLACES ▶ ADVICE ▶ A TOURIST DESTINATION ▶ CHOICES
▶ A DESCRIPTION OF A PLACE

7d To rent or to buy?

Real life stating preferences and giving reasons

1 Work in pairs. Write a checklist of things you should think about when you are looking for somewhere to live.

2 ▶ 58 Listen to a conversation at an estate agent's. Does the woman mention the things on your checklist? What four things does she specify?

3 ▶ 58 Look at the expressions for stating preferences. Listen to the conversation again. Complete the expressions.

> **▶ STATING PREFERENCES**
>
> I think I'd rather _____ than _____, for now anyway.
> I'd prefer _____, but not too _____.
> So, two bedrooms, and preferably with _____.
> Would you rather _____ places or _____ ones?
> To be honest, I prefer _____ to _____.
> I must say I prefer living _____.
> I haven't got a car. I prefer to _____ or _____.

4 Work in pairs. Can you remember the reasons for the speakers' preferences? Compare your ideas. Then check in the audioscript on page 97.

5 Pronunciation rising and falling intonation

a ▶ 59 Listen to this question. Notice how the intonation rises then falls.

Would you rather live in a town or a village?

b ▶ 60 Listen and repeat the questions.

1 Do you prefer playing football or basketball?
2 Would you rather have tea or coffee?
3 Do you prefer summer or winter?
4 Would you rather go by car or by bike?
5 Do you prefer maths or science?
6 Would you rather eat fish or meat?

c Work in pairs. Add at least six more pairs of items to the list in Exercise 5b. Take turns to ask and answer about your preferences.

6 Work in groups of three. Where would you rather live? Ask and answer questions using these ideas. Explain your reasons. Do you think your preferences will change in the future?

1 In a new house or an old one?
2 In a city or in a village?
3 In a town centre or in the suburbs?
4 At the coast or in the mountains?
5 In a historic area or a new development?

my life   ▶ PLACES   ▶ ADVICE   ▶ A TOURIST DESTINATION   ▶ CHOICES
▶ A DESCRIPTION OF A PLACE

7e A great place

Writing a description of a place

1 Read the text. Where do you think it's from? Choose one of the options (a–c).

   a a personal blog
   b an estate agent's website
   c a tourist information website

2 How does the writer describe these things?

> streets and buildings   shops   facilities
> local residents   atmosphere

Let's move to … Sandgate

Is it possible for a place to be too perfect?

1 Sandgate is in the heart of the city and like many other historic city-centre neighbourhoods, it has a lot of charm. The streets are picturesque, full of fascinating old shops in gorgeous buildings.

2 As there's so much to do within walking distance, you won't need to use a car very often. There's the usual variety of bars, restaurants, leisure centres, and so on that you'd expect in a city. For families, there are great parks (like Greenfields), an excellent public library and good schools close by.

3 As a person who lives in a city, I know that city people can often have a reputation for being cold and unfriendly. In Sandgate, however, there's a real sense of community. The locals, a mix of older residents and new arrivals, say it's almost like living in a village.

4 House prices are reasonable for this type of area and, really, Sandgate seems to be perfect both as a place to live in and a place to visit.

3 Writing skill organizing ideas

a Read the text again. Write the number of the paragraph (1–4) next to the heading. There is one extra heading.

   a What kind of place is Sandgate?
   b What are the bad points?
   c Overall opinion?
   d What kind of people live there?
   e What can you do there?

b Where is the best place in the text to include a paragraph with the extra heading from Exercise 3a?

Word focus *as* and *like*

4 Look at these two extracts from the text. Choose the correct option. Then find two more examples of *as* and *like* which have these meanings.

   1 … and like many other historic city-centre neighbourhoods, it has …
      It is similar to / It is many historic city-centre neighbourhoods.

   2 As a person who lives in a city, I know …
      I am similar to / I am a person who lives in a city.

5 Find two other examples of *as* and *like* in the text. Match the examples with these meanings.

   1 because
   2 for example

6 Complete the sentences with *as* and *like*.

   1 _____ a life-long resident of my town, I take pride in our community.
   2 I love modern shopping malls _____ this.
   3 It's ideal _____ a holiday destination.
   4 Our public library is _____ a palace.
   5 _____ all good cafés, the one in my village has a great atmosphere.
   6 The old buildings, _____ the town hall, are beautiful.

7 You are going to write a description of your own neighbourhood. Make notes using the headings in Exercise 3a. Use these words or your own ideas.

> a bit limited   a good range   close to …
> easy access to …   elegant   excellent   modern
> unfriendly   welcoming

8 Decide on the order of the paragraphs in your description. Then write about 150–200 words.

9 Use these questions to check your description.

   • Are your ideas clearly organized into paragraphs?
   • If you've included *as* or *like*, have you used them correctly?
   • Does your description give the reader a clear picture of your neighbourhood?

10 Read a description a classmate has written about their neighbourhood. Would you like to move there or not? Give your reasons.

7f The town with no wi-fi

Two satellite dishes in the USA

Before you watch

1 You're going to watch a video about a town in the USA that has no wi-fi or mobile phones. What would be the main change in your life if you didn't have wi-fi? Would it be good or bad?

2 The speakers in the video use American English. Match the American English terms with similar British English terms.

American English	British English
cell/cellular phone	city centre
Congress	Parliament
downtown	mobile phone
gasoline	petrol
store	shop

3 Key vocabulary

a Read the sentences. The words in bold are used in the video. Guess the meaning of the words.

1 Jack built his house to his own design – it's certainly **unique**!
2 I'd love to have a **telescope** to see the stars at night.
3 I can't call you from the beach because there's no phone **signal**.
4 The heavy traffic badly affects the city's **atmosphere**.
5 I've looked all over the house for the **cordless** phone, but I can't find it.

b Match the words in bold in Exercise 3a with these definitions.

a a piece of equipment that makes distant things seem closer
b radio waves which are sent or received
c special and different from any others
d the air in a certain place or area
e without a cable or wire attached to it

While you watch

4 ▶ **7.1** Watch the video. Complete the sentences with the names of the people you see.

Artie Barkley	Joyce Nelson
Karen O'Neil	Michael Holstine

1 _____ and _____ are residents of the quiet zone (QZ) in Green Bank, West Virginia.
2 _____ works as the Business Manager of the National Radio Astronomy Observatory (NRAO) in Green Bank.
3 _____ is the Site Director of the National Radio Astronomy Observatory (NRAO) in Green Bank.

5 Work in pairs. Discuss the questions.

1 What does *quiet zone* mean exactly?
2 What does the NRAO do in Green Bank?

6 ▶ **7.1** Watch the first part of the video (0.00–0.59) again. Check your ideas from Exercise 5. What do the people say?

1 Artie Barkley says he just listens to
_____ .
2 Michael Holstine says that to _____ the radio atmosphere, Congress created the National Radio Quiet zone.
3 Karen O'Neil says if you have a radio _____ in an area of lots of radio noise, the signal you're looking for is destroyed.

7 ▶ **7.1** Watch the second part of the video (1.00 to the end) again. Answer the questions.

1 Which ONE of these modern conveniences is it OK to use in Green Bank?

gasoline engines	cellular phones
diesel engines	automatic door
wi-fi modems	openers
cordless phones	digital cameras

2 Why would it be difficult to create a new radio quiet zone?

After you watch

8 Vocabulary in context

a ▶ **7.2** Watch the clips from the video. Choose the correct meaning of the words and phrases.

b Answer the questions in your own words. Then work in pairs and compare your answers.

1 How many world-class sportspeople can you name?
2 Have you ever met anyone who is just like someone you know?
3 What's life like in your community?

9 Work in pairs. Discuss the questions.

1 Do the residents of Green Bank seem happy to live there? Give your reasons.
2 How would you feel about living in a quiet zone like Green Bank?

diesel (n) /'diːzəl/ a type of fuel used in lorries and some cars
Milky Way (n) /ˌmɪlki 'weɪ/ the galaxy that contains our solar system
modern conveniences (n) /ˌmɒdən kənˈviːniənsəz/ objects that make our lives much easier
obliterated (adj) /əˈblɪtəreɪtəd/ completely destroyed or removed
optical (adj) /'ɒptɪkəl/ visual

UNIT 7 REVIEW AND MEMORY BOOSTER

Grammar

1 Look at the photo of rooftop golf. Then complete the text. Use comparative forms and patterns of adjectives and adverbs. Use the past simple and *used to* form of the verbs.

I've never heard of rooftop golf before. I suppose that as cities get ¹ _____ (big / big), people live a long way from golf courses. When I was a kid I ² _____ (live) in a block of flats with a basement car park. During the day, the car park ³ _____ (be) almost empty, so we ⁴ _____ (play) football there. Obviously, we played ⁵ _____ (well) on a real field and we couldn't kick the ball ⁶ _____ (as / hard / as) when we played outside, but we ⁷ _____ (not mind). Having the basement meant we could play ⁸ _____ (often). These days in cities, gyms seem to be ⁹ _____ (more / more / popular). I suppose people spend a lot of time sitting at desks or in cars. And ¹⁰ _____ (less / active) they are, ¹¹ _____ (healthy) they feel. Gyms have taken the place of open spaces in a lot of cities.

2 Answer the questions about the text in Exercise 1.

1 What are the advantages and disadvantages of playing football in the car park?
2 Why are gyms popular in cities?

3 Write comments about the photo with a comparative form or pattern of the adverb or adjective. Then compare your sentences with your partner.

1 hit the ball / on a normal golf course (carefully)
2 get / to the edge (close)
3 practise / want to (often)
4 play / up there (well)
5 reach the target / each day (accurately)
6 hit the ball / go (harder / further)

I CAN	
talk about past states and past habits (*used to*, *would*)	
compare things and describe a process of change (comparative adverbs, comparative patterns with adverbs and adjectives)	

Vocabulary

4 Which is the odd one out in each group? Why?

1 bricks, igloo, wood
2 run-down, skyscrapers, traffic
3 flat, house, neighbourhood
4 built-up, polluted, residents
5 garden, town, village

5 ≫ **MB** You are an estate agent with an important house to sell – your own. Make notes on your home and the area that it's in. Decide on a price. Then try to sell your home to one of your classmates.

I CAN	
talk about cities	
talk about places to live	

Real life

6 Choose the correct option. Then match the two parts of the exchanges.

1 A: *I'd rather / I prefer* to live on my own.
2 A: Where would you rather *go / to go*?
3 A: *I'd rather / I prefer* the country to the coast.
4 A: I prefer *living / live* near my family.
5 A: *I'd rather / I prefer* visit a few more places first.
6 A: *I'd rather / I'd prefer* a bigger kitchen.

a B: What's wrong with this flat?
b B: Are you looking for a flat-share?
c B: I can show you a fantastic beach house.
d B: This flat is nice. Are you going to take it?
e B: I don't fancy looking around the city centre.
f B: Are you going to live near your work?

7 ≫ **MB** Work in groups. Ask and answer questions about your preferences. Give reasons for your answers.

fruit or cake	rice or pasta
jazz or pop	snow or sun
mornings or evenings	spring or autumn

I CAN	
ask about preferences	
state preferences and give reasons	

Unit 8 Travel

Tourists take photos of an emperor penguin on the frozen Amundsen Sea in Antarctica.

FEATURES

22 Holidays and memories

Writers return to their roots

24 Walking for wildlife

Mike Fay: a personal approach to saving wild places

26 All aboard!

A report on global tourism

30 Questions and answers

A video about National Geographic Explorers' lives

1 Work in pairs. Look at the photo. Discuss the questions.

1 What kind of holiday do you think this is? Why?
2 Do you think the people do this kind of trip often? Why? / Why not?
3 Would you like to take a trip like this?

2 ▶ 61 Listen to three people talking about travel. Write the number of the speaker (1–3) next to the things they talk about.

being on planes	planning
business trips	a round-the-world trip
day trips	taking local buses and trains
delays	travelling for work
luggage	weekends away

3 ▶ 61 Listen again. Each speaker shares a travel tip. What are their tips? Discuss the tips with your partner.

4 Which countries or cities have you been to? Find people in your class who have had similar experiences to you.

A: *Have you been to Vietnam?*
B: *Yes, we had a holiday there last year.*
A: *Me too! Where did you go?*

my life ▶ HOLIDAY COMPANIONS ▶ FAVOURITE ACTIVITIES ▶ GOING GREEN ▶ TRAVEL PROBLEMS ▶ A TEXT MESSAGE

8a Holidays and memories

Vocabulary holiday activities

1 Work in pairs. Why did you choose the destination of your most recent holiday? Tell your partner.

saw the place on TV
followed a friend's recommendation
wanted to visit somewhere new
wanted to return to a place I know
went to visit family/friends

2 Work in pairs. Match the activities (1–6) with the examples (a–f). What do you enjoy doing when you go on holiday? Give your own examples.

1 taking it easy
2 going sightseeing
3 having new experiences
4 being active
5 learning new things
6 spending time with friends or family

a hiking in the mountains
b lying on the beach
c playing board games
d riding on a camel
e taking a painting course
f visiting famous monuments

Reading

3 Look at the photo with the article. Which of these things (a–c) do you think it shows?

a a coastline
b a market
c a village

4 Read the article and answer the questions.

1 Where are the writers from and what are their destinations?
2 Which writers haven't been to these places before?
3 Which writer has problems with the language?
4 Which writer travels with his/her parents?
5 Which writer has to change his/her plans? Why?

5 Which activities in Exercise 2 did the three writers do?

Holidays *and* memories

Three writers return to the lands their families came from

▶ 62

1 Lucy Chang
I step off the train in Taipei and follow the crowd into Shilin, one of the city's most famous night markets. Brightly-lit red, white and yellow signs are swinging above the market stalls. I'm not very good at reading Chinese characters, in spite of being from Taiwan originally. Stall holders call out to me. It's my first visit here and I'm too embarrassed to speak. Back home in London, I learned to say a few words, but right now my mind is blank. It's not a good start to my trip.

2 Liz Mullan
Arriving at Belfast International Airport is always emotional. It feels like home. We head north to some of Europe's highest ocean cliffs. After a couple of hours, we're standing on the Giant's Causeway. The wind almost blows us off the rocks into the North Atlantic Ocean. I look west towards home and imagine sailing across this wild ocean to Canada, like my great-grandfather did in 1890. We planned to walk along the coast like last time, but it's raining hard so we decide to find a café and hot food. Maybe tomorrow will bring the sun.

3 Frank Rossellini
When I was a child, my parents always promised to take me to Sicily one day. Finally, when they are both in their eighties, we have managed to get here. In this tiny village, we sit down to a dinner with lots of aunts, uncles and cousins. Eating together is still the most important part of the day here. After enormous plates of sausage, pasta, salads and homemade bread, everyone enjoys telling us stories of the friends and family members who left for New York decades earlier. It feels great to be here and I think about coming back again in the future.

Grammar verb patterns: *-ing* form and *to* + infinitive

> ▶ **VERB PATTERNS: *-ING* FORM and *TO* + INFINITIVE**
>
> ***-ing* form**
> *I imagine sailing across this wild ocean to Canada.*
> *Eating together is important.*
> *I'm not very good at reading Chinese characters.*
>
> ***to* + infinitive**
> *My parents always promised to take me to Sicily.*
> *I'm too embarrassed to speak.*
>
> For further information and practice, see page 86.

6 Look at the grammar box. Choose the correct option to complete these sentences. Then find an example of each use in the article.

1 We use the *-ing* form of the verb after certain verbs, as the subject of a sentence and after *adjectives / prepositions*.
2 We use the *to* + infinitive form of the verb after certain verbs and after *adjectives / prepositions*.

7 Each option in these sentences is grammatically possible but one option isn't true, according to the article. Which one?

1 Lucy Chang *described / finished / mentioned* going to the market.
2 Lucy Chang *needs / manages / wants* to speak Chinese.
3 Liz Mullan *adores / avoids / loves* going to Ireland.
4 Liz Mullan *expected / intended / threatened* to walk along the coast.
5 Frank Rossellini's parents *planned / refused / wanted* to travel to Sicily.
6 Frank Rossellini *fails / hopes / intends* to return to the village.

8 Choose the correct option to complete the sentences. Then work in pairs. Tell your partner which sentences you agree with.

1 *Travelling / To travel* by train is usually pleasant.
2 Good hotels are easy *finding / to find*.
3 *Cycling / To cycle* can be a good way of seeing a new city.
4 *Sleeping / To sleep* on a plane can be difficult.
5 Some hotels are too expensive *staying / to stay* in.
6 I'm interested in *trying / to try* new things on holiday.
7 *Going / To go* on holiday with friends is always fun.
8 I get fed up with *spending / to spend* every day on the beach.

9 ▶ 63 Complete the conversation with the *-ing* form and *to* + infinitive form of the verbs. Then listen and check.

Rose: Hi there, I'm Rose.
Matt: Hi, I'm Matt.
Rose: Is this your first time in Corfu?
Matt: No, actually. We come every year. We love ¹＿＿＿＿＿＿ (stay) here.
Rose: So do we. We keep ² ＿＿＿＿＿ (come) back year after year. It's hard ³ ＿＿＿＿ (find) somewhere with everything you need for a holiday – great beaches, fantastic weather and something for everyone to do.
Matt: I know. Actually, there's a paragliding class later – I fancy ⁴ ＿＿＿＿＿ (try) that.
Rose: My friends want ⁵ ＿＿＿＿＿ (do) that too! To be honest, ⁶ ＿＿＿＿＿ (lie) by the pool is my idea of a holiday.
Matt: Oh, I get a bit bored with ⁷ ＿＿＿＿ (do) that after the first day or two. I need ⁸ ＿＿＿＿＿ (move) around and do things.
Rose: Well, why not? It's a different way of ⁹ ＿＿＿＿＿ (relax), I suppose.
Matt: Yes, that's right. Well, if you decide ¹⁰ ＿＿＿＿＿ (go) paragliding with your friends, we'll see you there!

Listening and speaking ⟨ my life ⟩

10 ▶ 64 Listen to people talking about holidays and complete the sentences. Do you think they would be good holiday companions for you? Which person would you prefer to go on holiday with?

1 I enjoy … .
2 I quite fancy … .
3 I don't mind … .
4 I'd like … .
5 I can't afford … .
6 I'm quite keen on … .
7 I don't like … .
8 I'm interested in … .
9 I can't stand … .
10 I'm happy … .

11 Think about how you would complete the sentences in Exercise 10. Then talk to people in your class and find someone who would make a good holiday companion.

12 Work with your holiday companion and decide what kind of holiday to have. Tell the class:

- where and when you would go
- how you'd get there
- where you'd stay
- what you'd do there and why

8b Walking for wildlife

Mike Fay, *a conservationist whose work makes a difference*

- **trekked** 10,000 kilometres in Africa and North America

- **counted** giant redwood trees in North America, elephant populations in central Africa

- **created** 13 national parks in Gabon

- **protected** thousands of elephants from poachers

- **survived** a malaria attack, an elephant attack, a plane crash

- **flown** over the African continent for an aerial survey

- **uploaded** thousands of photos to Google Earth

- **helped** to create a marine park off the Gabon coast

poacher (n) /'pəʊtʃə/ someone who catches and kills animals illegally
survey (n) /'sɜːveɪ/ the measuring and recording of the details of an area of land
trek (v) /trek/ make a long and difficult journey

Listening

1 What kind of work does a conservationist do? What is their main aim?

2 Look at the information about Mike Fay. Do you think he's a typical conservationist? Why? / Why not?

   probably not, because he's trekked 10,000 kilometres and has had some dangerous/exciting experiences

3 ▶ 65 Listen to an extract from a radio programme about Mike Fay. Complete the sentences.

   1 Mike Fay's work is about saving the last .... on Earth.
   2 He's spent a total of more than .... years of his life on treks.
   3 His usual luggage is a T-shirt, a pair of shorts and a ....
   4 He's walked in Africa, the United States and ....
   5 He's worried about how .... people will affect the planet.

4 ▶ 65 Listen to the extract again and choose the correct option to complete the sentences.

   1 Recently, Fay has been *flying / walking* across Canada.
   2 Mining companies have been *looking for / producing* gold and oil.
   3 Mining companies have been *digging up / destroying* vast areas.
   4 In Gabon, people have been *asking / trying* to set up mines near parks.

5 Work in pairs. Would you like to spend a year working with Mike Fay? Why? / Why not?

Grammar present perfect simple and continuous

> **PRESENT PERFECT SIMPLE and CONTINUOUS**
>
> **Present perfect simple**
> *When you've walked across half of Africa and you've walked up the west coast of North America, where do you go next?*
> *They've destroyed hundreds of square kilometres of wilderness.*
>
> **Present perfect continuous**
> *Recently he's been walking again, this time across Canada.*
> *He hasn't been taking it easy!*
> *What has he been doing since then?*
> Stative verbs like *be, have, know, like* are not usually used in the continuous form.
>
> For further information and practice, see page 86.

6 Look at the grammar box. Answer the questions.

1 How do we form the present perfect simple? How do we form the present perfect continuous?
2 Which verb form emphasizes the duration or repetition of an activity? Which verb form emphasizes an action or an activity that is complete?

7 Complete the text with the present perfect simple and present perfect continuous form of the verbs.

> This year, Mike Fay [1] .... (work) in Gabon. He [2] .... (check) the situation in the national parks and he [3] .... (discover) some problems. For example, poachers [4] .... (kill) elephants again. Fay [5] .... (talk) about ways of controlling poaching with the Gabonese government. As a result, the Gabonese president [6] .... (send) soldiers to several of the parks. So far, the poachers [7] .... (not / return). Meanwhile, for the past few years, foreign ships [8] .... (fish) in the marine park. The Gabonese government [9] .... (try) to find ways of dealing with this problem.

8 Write questions for Mike Fay with the present perfect simple and present perfect continuous form of the verbs.

1 What / you / do / recently?
2 you / prepare for / any new trips?
3 How / you / feel / since the plane crash?
4 How many photos / you / take / in your career?
5 How long / you / travel / alone?
6 you / be / anywhere dangerous lately?

9 Match the travel preparation activities (1–6) with the results (a–f). Then write two sentences.

I've been buying holiday clothes. I've spent a fortune.

1 buy holiday clothes
2 look for cheap flights
3 talk to travel agents
4 download tourist information
5 pack my suitcase
6 practise useful phrases in Thai

a be on the phone all morning
b spend a fortune
c run out of space
d not learn many
e print a couple of pages
f not find any

Grammar *How long … ?*

> **HOW LONG … ?**
>
> *How long have you had this camera?*
> *How long have you been travelling alone?*
> *How long did it take you to get there?*
>
> For further information and practice, see page 86.

10 Look at the grammar box. Which verb form is used in each question? Why?

11 Match the questions (1–6) with the answers (a–e). Then work in pairs and continue the conversations.

1 How long have you been coming to this resort?
2 How long did the flight from London take?
3 How long have you known each other?
4 How long did you spend in Canada?
5 How long have you been waiting for the bus?
6 How long have you been here?

a About ten hours non-stop.
b For the last four or five years.
c I was there for a couple of months.
d Not long – we met on holiday this spring.
e Only a few minutes. But I think we just missed one.
f We arrived yesterday morning.

A: How long have you been coming to this resort?
B: For the last four or five years.
A: Has it changed a lot in that time?

Speaking ⟨ my life

12 What kinds of activities are you interested in? How long have you been doing them? Work in pairs and tell your partner. Ask follow-up questions. Use some of these ideas.

I've been … since/for …
I took it up when …
I've always/never …
In the last few … , I've …

8c All aboard!

Reading

1 Work in pairs. Discuss the questions.

1 Do many tourists come to your country or region? From which countries?
2 What do these tourists do? Activity holidays, backpacking, cultural sightseeing, ecotourism, or other holiday activities?
3 What are the advantages of this tourism? Are there any disadvantages?

2 Read the article quickly. What is it about? Choose the best option (a–c).

a It describes extreme activities tourists can do.
b It compares the positive and negative effects of tourism.
c It talks about the impact of lots of tourists on a destination.

3 Read the article again and complete the table.

Destination	Number of tourists	Impact
1	2 on a cruise ship	Falling numbers of 3
Himalayas: 4	5 in the climbing season	6 each year left on the mountain
7	8	Negative effects on 9

4 Answer the questions with information from the article.

1 When did the tourism industry start to be successful?
2 Why are cruises bad for the environment? Find three reasons.
3 What have groups been doing to improve the environment on Everest?
4 What action has the government of the Balearic Islands taken, and why?

5 Find these words in the article. Look at how the words are used and try to guess their meaning. Then complete the sentences (1–6).

pollution (line 11)   charge (line 37)
equipment (line 24)   challenges (line 39)
rubbish (line 26)   ecotourism (line 45)

1 Airlines usually _____ you a lot of money if your luggage is over the weight limit.
2 On average, each person in the UK produces about 500 kg of _____ each year.
3 I don't have much kitchen _____ – just a microwave.
4 Speaking a new language can be one of the hardest _____ when you travel abroad.
5 _____ is a way of enjoying a holiday without damaging the environment.
6 Plastic is a major cause of _____ in the oceans.

Critical thinking close reading

6 According to the article, are these statements true (T) or false (F)? Or is there not enough information (N) in the article to say if the statements are true or false?

1 The tourism industry has grown steadily and has now reached its peak.
2 There are fewer Magellanic penguins since cruises started visiting Patagonia.
3 Climbers on Everest cause problems for the local population.
4 There's not enough fresh water in the Balearic Islands in the holiday season.
5 It's better to stay at home than be an ecotourist.

7 Work in pairs. Underline the sections of the article that helped you decide about the sentences in Exercise 6. Do you agree with each other?

8 Work as a class. Discuss the questions.

1 Do you think an eco-tax on tourists is a good idea?
2 What is your answer to the final question in the article?

Speaking my life

9 Work in pairs. Look at these activities. Decide if they have a good or bad impact on the environment. Which ones does your family do?

1 flying to distant holiday destinations
2 recycling household waste (paper, glass, organic waste)
3 travelling by car
4 switching off lights and electrical appliances
5 saving water (turning off taps, not watering the garden)
6 using eco-friendly cleaning products

10 Work in groups. How easy is it for you and your family to live a green lifestyle?

A: We've been recycling paper for years. It's not hard to remember to do if you have a special box for it.
B: We do that too.

All — ABOARD!

A plane comes in to land on the Caribbean island of Saint Martin.

▶ 66

The tourism industry started to grow rapidly in the middle of the last century and it's been growing ever since. In the last twenty years especially, more and more people have been travelling to distant places around the world. It's a wonderful thing, to be able to travel to destinations we had previously only read about or seen on television. But what kind of impact do large numbers of
5 people have on these places?

A voyage to the end of the Earth?

A large cruise ship can carry as many as six thousand passengers at a time, with about twenty-four million people going on cruises every year. Cruise ships drop about ninety
10 thousand tons of waste into the oceans every year and each ship produces as much air pollution as five million cars. The effects of this are made even worse by the fact that cruises visit the same places over and over again, so the damage is repeated. In Patagonia, this has been having an effect on
15 wildlife. The numbers of Magellanic penguins have been falling for some years now, for example.

Climbing to the top of the world

Far fewer people go climbing or trekking in the Himalayas than take a cruise, but in the short climbing season each May
20 about a thousand people try to climb Everest. At times, there are actually queues of climbers on the route to the top. The difficult conditions mean that everyone needs to take a lot of equipment with them. Unfortunately, for the last few decades, climbers have been leaving their equipment on Everest. In
25 recent years, clean-up teams have been organizing expeditions just to pick up this rubbish. The teams are made up of local and international climbers. One group has brought over eight tons of rubbish down from the mountain!

Let's all go to the beach

30 What happens when a region of about a million people is visited by thirteen million tourists every year? The Balearic Islands in the Mediterranean Sea have been dealing with this situation for decades. Where has the fresh water, the food, the petrol and the electricity for thirteen million tourists
35 come from? And how have the islands maintained the quality of the beaches, the roads and the countryside? Recently, the government of the Balearic Islands decided to charge tourists an ecotax of two euros a day. This has been tried once before, but it wasn't a success. However, the challenges
40 have been getting harder every year. The money from the tax is used to reduce the negative effects of tourism on the local environment.

Difficult choices

So, should we travel or simply stay at home? Many destinations offer low-impact tourism such as ecotourism. It's time to ask
45 ourselves some difficult questions. Can we really visit the world's beautiful places without destroying them?

waste (n) /weɪst/ rubbish

8d Is something wrong?

Vocabulary travel problems

1 Work in pairs. Have you ever had any travel problems involving these things? Tell your partner. Which of these problems can a tour guide help you with?

baggage allowances	hotel rooms
boarding cards	passport control
car hire	train timetables
customs checks	travel documents
flight delays	travel sickness
food poisoning	

▶ **WORDBUILDING compound nouns (noun + noun)**

We can use two nouns together to mean one thing.
baggage allowance, car hire

For further practice, see Workbook page 67.

Real life dealing with problems

2 ▶ 67 Listen to two conversations between a tour guide and tourists. Write the number of the conversation (1 or 2) next to the problem they talk about.

a The person has missed his/her flight home.
b Someone has had an accident.
c The luggage hasn't arrived.
d The flight has been delayed.
e The person has lost his/her plane tickets.
f Someone is ill.

3 ▶ 67 Look at the expressions for dealing with problems. Can you remember who said what? Write G (guide) or T (tourist) next to the expressions. Then listen to the conversations again and check.

▶ **DEALING WITH PROBLEMS**

I wonder if you could help us?
Is anything wrong?
Can I help?

Our luggage hasn't arrived.
Which flight were you on?
How did that happen?
Do you know where our bags have gone to?
When's the next flight?
It's about my wife.
How long has she been feeling like this?
Is there anything you can do?

I'm afraid the luggage has gone to Rome.
Don't worry, we'll arrange everything.
I'll ask the hotel to send for a doctor.

4 Work as a class. Are the problems solved? How?

5 Pronunciation strong and weak forms

a ▶ 68 Look at the position of *to* in these sentences. Listen to the sentences. In which sentence is *to* strong /tuː/? In which one is it weak /tə/?

1 Do you know which airport our bags have gone to?
2 Yes, I'm afraid the luggage has gone to Rome.

b ▶ 69 Listen and repeat these questions. Use strong or weak forms of *at, from* and *for*. Then work in pairs. Ask the questions and give your own answers.

1 Which hotel are you staying at?
2 Are you staying at the Ocean Hotel?
3 Where have you travelled from?
4 Why haven't we heard from the airline?
5 What have we been waiting for?
6 Are you waiting for the manager?

6 Work in pairs. Choose one of the conversations from Exercise 2. Take a role each. Look at the audioscript on page 98 and prepare your role. Then close your books and practise the conversation.

7 Take the roles of a tourist and a tour guide. Choose from the problems in Exercise 2 and act out two conversations. Use the expressions for dealing with problems to help you.

8e Hello from London!

Writing a text message

1 Read the message from Lynne. Answer the questions.

1. Where has Lynne come from and where is she now?
2. Who do you think the message is for? Friends, family, or both?
3. What does Lynne say about the people and the city?
4. What has she been doing?

Hi everyone!
Finally made it to London after 18-hour delay in Bangkok!!! 😰 Weather here awful but people fantastic. London massive compared to Brisbane! So far have: been shopping in Oxford Street, seen the Shard (wow!), done the Harry Potter tour (awesome!), had a boat trip along the river. Then slept all day & night cos jetlagged 😫. Text from my uncle in Edinburgh – he's found me a job there for summer! Spk soon L xx 😋

2 Writing skill informal style

a Read the message again. Which of these features of informal style does Lynne use?

abbreviations	informal expressions
comments in brackets	listing items
contractions	missing out words
exclamation marks	symbols

b Look at this extract from the message. The words *I* and *an* are missing. Mark their position in the complete sentence.

Finally made it to London after 18-hour delay in Bangkok!!!

c Mark the places in the message where Lynne has missed out words. What are the words?

d Rewrite the sentences in full.

1. city massive & noisy!
2. not got theatre tickets cos fully booked
3. been visiting Tower of London – scary!
4. took selfies (lots) on Oxford St
5. can't understand London accent (trying!)
6. text from Jo – arriving Sunday

e Rewrite the sentences. Miss out words where possible.

1. The weather is wet and it has been very cold sometimes.
2. I've been touring all the typical places – it's exhausting!
3. The people here are very kind and they have helped me a lot.
4. I took some photos of some pigeons – they're everywhere!
5. I haven't heard anything from Anton yet.
6. I'm getting a bus up to Edinburgh because flying is too expensive.

3 Choose a place you have visited or would like to visit. Make notes. Use the questions in Exercise 1 as a guide.

4 Decide who to write to. Write a message of about 75 words describing your trip. Use some of the features of informal style from Exercise 2a and miss out words which are not necessary.

5 Send your message to someone in your class. Then read the message you have received. Use these questions to check your classmate's message.

- Is everything clearly expressed?
- Are there any sections you do not understand?

6 Work in pairs. Tell your partner about the message you have received.

A: I got a message from Daisuke the other day.
B: Oh! How's he getting on?

8f Questions and answers

Cory Richards on the Cordillera Blanca in Peru

Before you watch

1 You're going to watch two videos in which National Geographic Explorers give their personal answers to questions. Before you watch, discuss these questions.

1 What kind of work do explorers do? Where do they work?
2 What items might they need to take with them when they're exploring?
3 Why do you think people become explorers?

2 Key vocabulary

a Read the sentences. The words in bold are used in the video. Guess the meaning of the words.

1 If you want to watch animals in the wild, a pair of **binoculars** is very useful.
2 I'd get really burned if I didn't use **sunblock**.
3 I'm not very good with a **paintbrush** – I prefer doing pencil drawings.
4 All children are **curious** about the world around them.
5 I've been making good **progress** in Italian since I started classes.

b Match the words in bold in Exercise 2a with these definitions.

a a tool to paint with
b cream that protects your skin from the sun
c equipment with lenses for looking at things far away
d improvement and development
e interested in something and wanting to learn about it

While you watch

Video 1: What item would you not leave home without?

3 Read what four of the explorers say about why they chose the items they take with them. What do you think they are talking about?

1 Carlton Ward, photographer
'without a _____, we'd still be paddling in circles somewhere'
2 Amy Dickman, zoologist
'_____, just to have a break at the end of the day'
3 Chris Thornton, archaeologist
'_____. I'm very, very white.'
4 Cory Richards, photographer
'a _____ to record what I'm experiencing'

4 ◻ 8.1 Watch the video. Check your ideas from Exercise 3.

5 ◻ 8.1 Watch the video again. Tick the items the explorers mention.

binoculars   camera   DVDs
family photographs   GPS   hat   headlamp
knife   local person   paintbrush   pencil
sunblock   sunglasses

6 Work in pairs. Which of the items in Exercise 5 surprised you? Did the explorers mention any of the items you discussed in Exercise 1 question 2?

Video 2: Why is it important to explore?

7 ◻ 8.2 Read what the explorers in the video say. What do you think the missing word is? Then watch the video and check your ideas.

1 John Francis, ecologist
'If you have _____ and you don't pursue them, then to me it's a life unlived.'
2 Laly Lichtenfeld, big cat conservationist
'It keeps _____ exciting, I mean that's what exploring is about.'
3 Enric Sala, marine ecologist
'Without exploration, there would be no _____.'
4 Lee Berger, paleoanthropologist
'We think we _____ how things work, but we don't.'

8 ◻ 8.2 Watch the video again. Who gave the most interesting answer, in your opinion?

After you watch

9 Vocabulary in context

a ◻ 8.3 Watch the clips from the videos. Choose the correct meaning of the words and phrases.

b Answer the questions in your own words. Then work in pairs and compare your answers.

1 Does the power ever go out where you live? What do you do when that happens?
2 Do you think it's human nature to be curious? What else is human nature?
3 What kind of thing do you think drives artists and business people?

10 Work in pairs. Discuss the questions.

1 What would you not leave home without if you were travelling?
2 Why is it a good idea to travel?

---

engage (v) /ɪnˈɡeɪdʒ/ to keep your interest or hold your attention
fundamentally (adv) /fʌndəˈmentəli/ basically, most importantly
paddle (v) /ˈpædəl/ to move a boat with an oar
pursue (v) /pəˈsjuː/ to follow or work at

Grammar

1 Complete the article about Thomas Cook with the correct verb tense or form. Use the following: past simple, present perfect simple, present perfect continuous, -ing form or infinitive with to.

Before 1872, people [1] _____ (not / travel) for pleasure very much. Then a man called Thomas Cook [2] _____ (change) everything when he [3] _____ (form) a travel agency, Thomas Cook & Son. Cook aimed [4] _____ (provide) educational and cultural tours. His son was successful in [5] _____ (expand) the business around the world. At first, foreign travel was expensive, but incomes [6] _____ (rise) since those days. Nowadays, many millions of ordinary people expect [7] _____ (go) on holiday at least once a year. In the twentieth century, holiday makers preferred [8] _____ (book) trips with travel agencies. For the last few years, travel agencies [9] _____ (struggle) because most people [10] _____ (make) their own plans online. Thomas Cook, however, is still one of the biggest travel companies in the world.

2 Answer the questions about the article in Exercise 1.

1 How has travel changed since the time of Thomas Cook?
2 Why do you think the travel agency *Thomas Cook & Son* was successful?

3 **›› MB** Write four true or false sentences about yourself with these verbs. Work in pairs and say if your partner's sentences are true or false.

have been learning	have seen
am interested in trying	want to go

I CAN
use verb patterns correctly (-ing form and to + infinitive) ☐
talk about recent activities and experiences (present perfect simple and continuous) ☐

4 **›› MB** Work in pairs. Have you ever been to places like these on holiday? Ask and answer questions about your experiences.

a beach resort	a safari
a cultural centre	a theme park
a natural park	a zoo

Vocabulary

5 Match nouns from A and B to make travel vocabulary. Then write questions with the expressions.

A		B	
baggage	flight	allowance	control
boarding	passport	card	delays
customs	travel	checks	sickness

6 **›› MB** Work in pairs. Which of these activities would you do in a seaside resort, a big city, a natural park and a campsite? Give your reasons.

be active	learn new things
go sightseeing	spend time with friends
have new	or family
experiences	take it easy

I CAN
use travel vocabulary appropriately ☐
talk about holiday activities ☐

Real life

7 Read these sentences from a conversation at an airport. Put the sentences (a–h) in order (1–8).

a A: What? How has that happened?
b A: Well, let's have another look. Calm down.
c A: Well, have you looked through all your pockets?
d A: Is anything wrong?
e B: Yes, I have. And I've checked the suitcase.
f B: I've been worrying so much about everything, and now this!
g B: I think I've lost the boarding passes.
h B: I don't know. I thought they were in my pocket, but they aren't there now.

8 **›› MB** Work in pairs. Act out conversations similar to Exercise 7.

Conversation 1: Student A is a tourist and Student B is a tour guide. Student A has lost his/her passport.

Conversation 2: Student A is an airline official and Student B is a customer. The flight is cancelled.

I CAN
talk about travel problems ☐
ask for and give explanations ☐

Unit 9 Shopping

Galleria Vittorio Emanuele, Milan, Italy

FEATURES

34 Shopping trends

How do you do your shopping?

36 Spend or save?

Do you buy on impulse?

38 The art of the deal

How to negotiate a price

42 Making a deal

A video about shopping in the oldest market in Morocco

1 Work in pairs. Look at the photo and the caption. Compare this place with places you usually go shopping.

2 ▶ 70 Listen to a market researcher interviewing some people who are shopping. Complete the table.

Interview	What?	Who for?
1	the latest	....
2	a couple of	himself
3	some	each other

3 Discuss the questions with your partner. Use the ideas in the box to help you.

books/DVDs/CDs	shoes
clothes	toiletries/cosmetics
electronics/gadgets	other items
jewellery	

1 What's the best (or worst) present anyone has ever given you?
2 What kind of things do you and your family or friends buy for each other?
3 Do you buy these things for yourself?

4 Work in pairs. Prepare a survey on shopping habits. Ask at least three other people your questions. Then compare the results.

9a Shopping trends

Reading

1 Work in pairs. How do you prefer to do your shopping? Tell your partner and give reasons.

> at markets (indoor or outdoor)
> in department stores
> in malls or shopping centres
> in small local shops
> online

2 Read what a farmer and a store manager say about selling their products. Answer the questions.

1. What kind of products do they talk about?
2. What kind of shopping do they talk about?
3. Where do they sell their products?

3 Read the article again. Find one advantage to customers and one to sellers for each kind of shopping.

4 Work in pairs. Can you think of any disadvantages to each kind of shopping?

Shopping trends
in the UK

▶ 71

Gilly McGregor
Yorkshire farmer

'Farmers' markets are the traditional way of selling food, but they disappeared for a few years in the UK. Now they're coming back. I have a stall in the town centre four days a week. When I sell directly to the consumers, they pay less and I still get a good price. That's because the vegetables don't have to be packaged and I don't have to pay a wholesaler to distribute and sell my products. The customers are happy because the vegetables are fresher and better quality than in the supermarket, so they keep for longer. A lot of supermarket stuff has to be eaten within a couple of days.'

Mark Noble,
manager at LowCo Stores

'These days, lots of people have busy lives and we have found that online shopping is a growing area for us. It's especially popular with people who buy the same things in the same amounts every week. At first, online shopping was used mainly by our regular customers, but since we introduced our mobile phone app, more new accounts have been set up. Once the customer makes their online list, it can be used again and again or it can be changed very easily.

Food and household items are delivered to the customers' homes for a small charge, or people can collect them in the store. In that case, the order must be collected the next day. A new order tracking app is being developed at the moment, and with that we'll be able to improve our service to customers even more.'

> **wholesaler** (n) /ˈhəʊlseɪlə/ a company that buys products in large quantities from the maker and sells them to different shops

Grammar passives

5 Look at the grammar box. Find a simple passive, a modal passive and a continuous passive. Then answer the questions.

1 How do we form the passive? Think about the auxiliary verb and the form of the main verb.
2 What kind of information follows the word *by*?

6 Underline six more passive forms in the article *Shopping trends in the UK*. Does the use of the passive emphasize the action or the person who does the action?

7 Choose the correct options to complete the text about a company that sells coffee.

We started direct trade about four years ago. This means that more of the final price ¹ *pays / is paid* to the growers. We have a simple system. First, the coffee beans ² *take / are taken* to a central collection point by each grower. When the loads ³ *have weighed / have been weighed*, the growers ⁴ *get / are got* the correct payment. At the moment, we ⁵ *are using / are being used* a standard shipping company to transport the coffee to Europe. But we ⁶ *are reviewing / are being reviewed* our arrangements and next year, probably, specialized firms ⁷ *will contract / will be contracted* to handle shipping. Once in Europe, the coffee ⁸ *can pack and sell / can be packed and sold* within a week.

8 Work in pairs. Write the passive form of the verbs.

1 Since its launch in 2003, 250 million *Nokia 1101 mobile phones / Apple iPods* _____ (sell).
2 With 400 shops around the world, clothing brand *Ralph Lauren / Mango* _____ (wear) by more people than any other.
3 The work of *J.K. Rowling / Agatha Christie* _____ (translate) into more languages than any other author.
4 In 1986, the film *The Color Purple / Out of Africa* _____ (nominated) for eleven Oscars but didn't win any.
5 *Solitaire / Tetris* _____ (adapt) for 65 different systems, making it the most successful computer game ever.
6 The first music video by *Justin Bieber / Lady Gaga* _____ (view) on YouTube over 500 million times.
7 Maps for the Xbox® game *Call of Duty / Grand Theft Auto* _____ (download) one million times in 24 hours when it went on sale.
8 A painting by *Picasso / Van Gogh* _____ (buy) at auction for $106 million in 2010.

9 ▶ 72 Underline the options you think are correct in Exercise 8. Then listen and check. How many answers did you get right?

Speaking 〈my life〉

10 Work in pairs. Find out about shopping now and in the future.

Student A: Turn to page 81 and follow the instructions.

Student B: Turn to page 82 and follow the instructions.

11 Work in groups of four. You are the makers of a new bag for people of your own age group. Decide on the following details for your bag. Find images online or make your own.

- what it will be/look like
- where/how it will be made
- where/how it will be sold
- who it will be aimed at
- how much it will cost
- why people should buy it

12 Present your product to the class. Vote on the one you'd most like to buy.

9b Spend or save?

Vocabulary shopping (1)

1 Work in pairs. Have you ever bought anything on impulse? Tell your partner about it.

2 Match the beginnings of the sentences (1–8) with the endings (a–h). Check the meaning of any words in bold you are not sure about.

1 The **checkout** is where you go
2 When things are on **special offer**,
3 At some supermarkets they help you
4 Fridges, washing machines and TVs
5 You can often get good **deals**
6 Cheap and expensive items
7 It isn't a good idea to
8 A **budget** is a way of working out

a are electrical **goods**.
b buy things that you can't **afford**.
c can both be good **value for money**.
d how much money you can spend.
e on products **in the sales**.
f the price is lower.
g to pack your **purchases**.
h to pay for your shopping.

3 Work in pairs. Ask and answer questions with the words in bold in Exercise 2.

*A: How do you choose which **checkout** queue to join at the supermarket?*
B: I usually look and see how much stuff people have in their trolleys.

Listening

4 ▶ **73** Listen to an extract from a radio programme that discusses what's in the news. Tick the examples of impulse buying which are mentioned.

1 Buying loads of things when you only need bread or milk.
2 Buying things you can't afford to buy.
3 Buying things online.
4 Spending too much when you're hungry.

5 ▶ **73** Listen to the extract again. Correct factual errors in four of the sentences.

1 Samira has written articles on impulse buying.
2 Most of us have spent more than £500 on a purchase that wasn't necessary!
3 You never see special offers on TVs or tablets.
4 You should always have a budget when you need to buy expensive things.
5 Many women, but few men, use shopping as a way of managing their money.
6 If you make a list, you can avoid impulse buying.

6 Work in pairs. Think of three ways people can control their impulse buying.

Grammar articles and quantifiers

▶ **ARTICLES**

1 *They're based on a study by* **the BBC.**
2 **The study** *divided people into two groups – men and women.*
3 *... plan your shopping and you'll save* **money.**
4 *So I just need to make sure I have* **a snack** *before I go?*

For further information and practice, see page 88.

7 Look at the words in bold in the grammar box. Which article (*a/an, the* or zero article) is used when:

a we mention something for the first time?
b we mention something which is known (because it has already been mentioned, for example)?
c there is only one of something?
d we are talking about something in general?

8 Read the ideas for saving money. Complete the sentences with the correct article (*a/an, the* or zero article).

TOP *Saving Tips*

1 Save your small change in _____ jar.
2 Unplug _____ electrical appliances when you're not using them.
3 Buy _____ products that are close to their sell-by date.
4 Don't get _____ credit card. If you have one, cut it up.
5 Compare _____ prices before you buy _____ expensive item.
6 Keep _____ receipts you get and add up _____ amount of money you spend every day.
7 Take _____ lunch from home instead of buying _____ sandwiches or _____ snacks.
8 Don't buy _____ books – borrow them from _____ library.

▶ **QUANTIFIERS**

1 *Several websites have articles about impulse buying.*
2 *If we can save* **a bit of** *money, that's good.*
3 *... come back with* **loads of** *things you hadn't intended to buy.*
4 *... you're more likely to buy* **loads of** *food.*

For further information and practice, see page 88.

9 Look at the grammar box. Answer the questions.

1 Look at sentences 1 and 2. Which quantifier is used with:
   a a countable noun?
   b an uncountable noun?
2 Look at sentences 3 and 4. When do we use the quantifier *loads of*?

10 Look at the audioscript on pages 98 and 99. Find nine more quantifiers and say if they are used with countable nouns, uncountable nouns or both.

11 Choose the correct quantifier. Then suggest another possible quantifier for each sentence.

1 I don't think I need to go shopping. We've got *plenty of / many* food for the week.
2 I've bought *a couple of / a bit of* magazines. I can read them on the train.
3 I didn't find *much / any* shoes in my size in the sales.
4 If I've got *a little / one or two* money at the end of the month, I buy something nice.
5 I bought *a few / some* strange cheese at the shops. It's almost green!
6 You can save *several / loads of* money if you shop in the sales.

12 Pronunciation linking

a ▶ **74** Listen to these sentences from Exercise 11. Notice how the speaker links the words which start with a vowel to the final consonant of the previous word.

1 I don't think‿I need to go shopping.
2 I can read them‿on the train.

b ▶ **75** Underline the words which start with vowels in the other sentences in Exercise 11. Then listen and repeat the sentences.

Speaking ⌐ my life⌐

13 Work in pairs. Make true (or false) sentences with these quantifiers about things you own, have bought or have been given. Tell your partner and ask follow-up questions.

a bit of	a couple of	a few	loads of
one or two	plenty of	several	some

A: I've got **a bit of** *wood I found on the beach.*
B: Have you? Why did you decide to keep it?

9c The art of the deal

Reading

1 Work in pairs. Do you like bringing souvenirs back from holiday? Discuss why you think people would bring back items like these.

> brochures from galleries, museums, etc.
> decorative objects: pictures, ceramics, etc.
> duty-free goods
> locally made products
> postcards
> T-shirts with slogans
> used tickets

2 Read the article quickly. Decide what kind of shopping experience (a–c) the article describes.

a buying crafts direct from the maker
b choosing holiday gifts for friends and family
c looking for bargains in local markets

3 Read the article again. Answer the questions.

1 Who are the three main people in the article and why do they go to Morocco?
2 What two things does Sam buy and how much does he pay for them?
3 Which is Sam's most successful purchase?

4 Look at the words (1–8). Find the things that are described with these words in the article. Complete the phrases. Then think of more things that can be described using these words.

1 beautiful old _____
2 world-famous _____
3 freshly-squeezed _____
4 deadly-looking _____
5 hand-dyed _____
6 massive copper _____
7 tall blue _____
8 bright yellow, Moroccan _____

Wordbuilding compound adjectives

▶ **WORDBUILDING compound adjectives**

Compound adjectives are adjectives made of more than one word. The hyphen shows that the words form one adjective.
duty-free goods, two-day lemon festival

For further practice, see Workbook page 75.

5 Look at the wordbuilding box. Then work in pairs. Answer the questions.

1 The *world-famous marketplace* is 'famous around the world'. What do the other compound adjectives in Exercise 4 mean?
2 Can you name examples of:
   a a well-known sportsperson?
   b a best-selling singer?
   c old-fashioned clothes?
   d a hand-made item?

Critical thinking testing a conclusion

6 The writer concludes: 'Mohamed will be proud.' Look at the article again and underline the pieces of advice Mohamed gives to Sam.

7 Tick the pieces of advice that Sam follows. How effective was the advice? How do you know?

Speaking ⟨ my life ⟩

8 Work in pairs. Describe typical souvenirs that people take home from your country.

9 You are a market trader. Choose four of these objects. Find or draw a picture of each object and think how you will describe it. Think about: its origin, age and material, and any interesting facts about it. Decide on a price for each object.

> boomerang bottle box clock coin figure
> hat lamp rug stamp sword watch

10 Choose objects from Exercise 9 which you want to buy. Visit different traders and find out about the objects you want. Then choose which trader you will buy from.

This rug is lovely. How much is it?

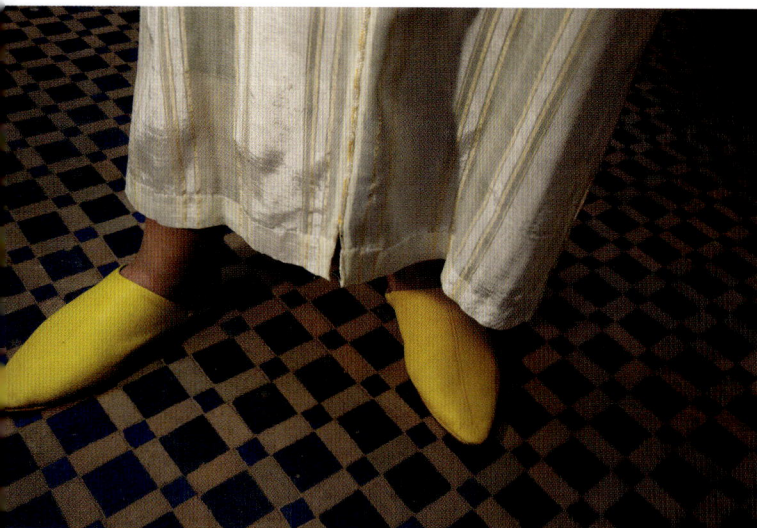

The *Art of the Deal*

by Andrew McCarthy

▶ 76

I'M IN MARRAKECH, the bustling heart of Morocco, with my son, Sam. He's eight. We've come here with Mohamed, a friend who owns a shop in our neighbourhood in New York. Sam can often be found in Mohamed's shop, looking for a bargain.
5   They argue about prices and chat about swords, or camels or the desert. 'You need to come to Morocco, to Marrakech,' Mohamed told me. 'I'll show you around and teach Sam how to really get a bargain!' So here we are.
   We meet up with Mohamed over a cup of mint tea in the
10 beautiful old city of Marrakech. We're sitting in an area next to the exotic stalls of the souk – Marrakech's world-famous marketplace. Market sellers with carts offer freshly-squeezed juice, others sell dates or figs. Later, as we wander around, Mohamed introduces us to olive sellers, tile makers and rug merchants. He also begins the
15 first of his lessons in bargaining for Sam.
   'The price of everything in Morocco is open to discussion, Sam. When you hear a price, the first thing you say is "Too much – *bezaf*" and then walk away.'
   'But what if I like it?'
20 'When you see something you like, maybe a lamp, you ask about something else instead. Then, as you walk out, you ask, "And how much is that lamp?" as though you'd just noticed it and aren't really that interested in it.'
   We turn a corner into another narrow street in the souk. 'Don't
25 always give an offer. Make them continue to lower the price. Oh, and wear something Moroccan,' Mohamed continues as we enter a fairly large shop. Most of the stalls in Marrakech sell mainly one type of thing, but not this one. Decorative and deadly-looking swords hang beside soft hand-dyed fabrics; large camel
30 bones covered in writing sit beside massive copper lamps. It is here that Sam spots a beautiful box. 'Look, a treasure chest!' It's made of wood, and painted red and gold. He opens the lid, then closes it. 'Cool.' Then he spots a tall blue bottle – an old perfume bottle. 'Four hundred dirham,' the shopkeeper says. Fifty dollars.

Sam says nothing. I can't tell whether he's too shy or is practising   35
what Mohamed has taught him.
He eventually agrees to pay 200 dirham, about $24. I'd say the bottle is worth $10, at most. Clearly, he needs more practice at this. 'Just to get started, Dad,' Sam tells me as he pays for the bottle.   40
We spend a few days sightseeing around Marrakech, but Sam is really interested in only one thing. Late one afternoon, we return to the shop where Sam saw the treasure chest. 'You have returned. Very good.' The shopkeeper opens his arms. He places the chest on the floor. Sam opens the lid. He runs his fingers over it.   45
The shopkeeper speaks. 'Give me 2,500.'
Sam shakes his eight-year-old head. 'Eight hundred.'
'I like your *babouches*,' says the man. Sam's wearing a pair of bright yellow, Moroccan slippers. He ignores the comment.
'You're very good. I'll take 1,800 dirham,' the shopkeeper   50
announces.
'One thousand.'
Both are silent. Neither blinks. What happens next happens fast.
'Fifteen hundred, and it's yours.'
'Twelve hundred.'   55
'Thirteen hundred.'
'Yes!'
The man holds out his hand. Sam grabs it. The deal is done. Mohamed will be proud.

---

bargain (n) /ˈbɑːgɪn/ something which has a low price but is good quality
blink (v) /blɪŋk/ open and close your eyes very quickly
bustling (adj) /ˈbʌslɪŋ/ energetic and busy
souk (n) /suːk/ the name in some countries for a market that sells all types of products

9d It's in the sale

Real life buying things

1 ▶ 77 Listen to two conversations. Answer the questions for each conversation.

1 What kind of shop is it?
2 What does the customer want?
3 Does the customer buy the item?

2 ▶ 77 Look at the expressions for buying things. Listen to the conversations again. Underline the option the speaker uses. Identify the speakers. Write C (customer) or A (assistant) next to the expressions.

> ▶ **BUYING THINGS**
>
> Can I have a look at / Could I see this silver chain?
> It's in the sale / It's reduced actually. It's got 20 per cent off.
> I wanted / I was looking for something lighter.
> Can she bring it back / return it if she doesn't like it?
> Excuse me, are you in / do you work in this department?
> What's / Do you have the reference number or the model name?
> Let me see if it's in stock / we've got any on order.
> How much do you charge / does it cost for delivery?
> We accept payment / You can pay by card or in cash.

Vocabulary shopping (2)

3 Work in pairs. Can you remember the question and response for each word? Check your answers in the audioscript on page 99.

> return   exchange   receipt   gift-wrapping
> reference number   model name   in stock   available
> delivery   tills

4 Pronunciation silent letters

a ▶ 78 Listen to these words. Notice how the crossed-out letter is silent. Repeat the words.

> gift-wrapping   receipt   right
> though

b ▶ 79 Say these words and cross out the silent letters. Then listen and check.

> answer   autumn   bought   design
> friendly   hour   listen   weigh

5 Work in pairs. Choose one of the conversations from Exercise 1. Take a role each. Look at the audioscript on page 99 and prepare your role. Then close your books and practise the conversation.

6 Take the roles of a customer and a shop assistant. Choose two of these items and act out two conversations. Use the expressions for buying things to help you.

> an item of furniture for your new home
> clothes for your father on his birthday
> toiletries for your sister
> a DVD for a friend
> a kitchen appliance for your brother
> sportswear for yourself

9e For sale

Writing customer feedback

1 Work in pairs. Do you read customer feedback when you buy things online? Have you ever changed your mind about a purchase after reading feedback?

2 Read the customer feedback from two online shopping sites. Answer the questions.

1 Which feedback is about a product and which is about a seller?
2 What problems do the customers mention?
3 Is the feedback positive or negative?

★★★★★

I have no hesitation in recommending PetTown. I ordered two identity tags, but after two weeks **they** hadn't arrived. When I emailed the company, **they** immediately sent replacement tags via registered mail at no extra charge. **They** were courteous and efficient and I would buy from **them** again.

★★★★☆

Bought this lovely shirt with an even lovelier 20% off. I wasn't disappointed. Great quality material and **it**'s a perfect fit. Good for work and for social occasions. Slightly surprised when washed with other items, **they** came out pale blue! This is the first time **it**'s happened with your products, however, and is the only reason I'm not giving **it** full marks. I do recommend the product, but care must be taken when washing.

3 Writing skill clarity: pronouns

a You can avoid repetition of nouns in your writing by using pronouns – as long as it is clear which noun each pronoun refers to. Look at the pronouns in bold in the customer feedback. What do they refer to?

b Read the sentences. Replace the nouns with pronouns to avoid repetition.

1 I felt that the colours of the rug in the online photo weren't accurate. The colours of the rug were much darker than I expected.
2 Two of the glasses were broken on arrival and we had to send all the glasses back.
3 My daughter received this game as a gift. My daughter loves the game.
4 This seller has always provided an excellent service and I'm happy to recommend the seller.

c Read the sentences. What do the pronouns refer to? If the sentence is not clear, replace the pronoun with a noun.

1 I bought the grey jacket and the black jumper online. When it came, I wasn't happy with the quality.
2 I ordered the books for delivery, but they missed my postcode off the address label.
3 The tracking information said the packet had been sent, but it never arrived.
4 I provided my address and a phone number. The courier said he couldn't find it.

4 Prepare customer feedback for something you have bought or about a seller. It can be an online or a shop purchase. Use these headings and make notes where relevant. Decide how many stars to give and if you recommend the product or seller.

- item
- delivery
- condition
- fit/quality
- standard of service

5 Write your recommendation. Use these questions to check your advert.

- Have you used pronouns clearly?
- Is your feedback useful to other customers?

6 Publish your feedback in the classroom. Read the other feedback comments and find out if anyone has had a similar shopping experience.

9f Making a deal

In Morocco's oldest market – the souk in Fez

Before you watch

1 Look at the photo and the caption. Discuss the questions.

   1 What's happening in the photo?
   2 Why do you think both men are smiling?
   3 What kind of things do you think you can buy in the souk?

2 Key vocabulary

a Read the sentences. Try to guess the missing words.

   1 When you buy things in the sales, you can often get really good _____ on the prices.
   2 I'm just going to look at the stuff in the market. I have no _____ of buying anything.
   3 We'll need to take two taxis – there are eight of us and the _____ for a taxi is five passengers.
   4 The hotel tried to _____ us – they charged us for four nights instead of three!
   5 The price of the bus hire is _____ . It's the same if we have ten people or twenty.

b Read the words in bold and their definitions. The words are used in the video. Complete the sentences in Exercise 2a with the words.

   a **cheat** (v) to be dishonest
   b **discounts** (n) reductions in price
   c **fixed** (adj) can't be changed
   d **intention** (n) plan
   e **maximum** (n) top limit

3 Which is bigger, a half or an eighth? Put the amounts in order of size, starting with the smallest.

a half	a sixth	an eighth
a quarter	a third	

While you watch

4 ◀ 9.1 Watch the first part of the video (0.00–0.53) with the sound OFF. Make a note of the things that you see for sale. Make a whole-class list and compare that with your ideas from Exercise 1 question 3.

5 ◀ 9.1 Watch the first and second parts of the video (0.00–2.41) with the sound ON. Answer the questions.

   1 What's the name of the small red hat described in the video?
   2 Complete what these people say about bargaining in the souk with words from Exercises 2 and 3.
      a Vincent (Dutch tourist): You have to start yourself at one _____ or something,
      b Consuela (Dutch tourist): So, then you get at _____ the price they say at first.
      c Ahmed (Tour guide): We don't really have a _____ price.
   3 What does Mohcine, the jewellery seller, say about some customers?

6 ◀ 9.1 Watch the third part of the video (2.42 to the end). Choose the correct option to complete the answers.

   1 What happens if a customer says they don't want to buy anything?
      The seller offers *a lower price / a different item.*
   2 What should all tourists make sure they don't do?
      They shouldn't *pay more than something is worth / buy too many things.*

After you watch

7 Work in pairs. How do you think the tourists felt about their experiences in the souk? Give reasons for your answers.

8 Vocabulary in context

a ◀ 9.2 Watch the clips from the video. Choose the correct meaning of the words and phrases.

b Complete the sentences in your own words. Then work in pairs and compare your sentences.

   1 I like face-to-face classes because …
   2 What a great present! Believe me, it's …
   3 I like to go step by step when …

9 Do you prefer bargaining or fixed prices? Give your reasons.

craftsman (n) /ˈkrɑːftsmən/ someone who makes quality items by hand
dates (n) /deɪts/ a kind of fruit that grows on palm trees
dirham (n) /ˈdɪəˈræm/ the money used in Morocco
haggling (n) /ˈhæglɪŋ/ bargaining, discussing a price to come to an agreement
vendors (n) /ˈvendəz/ sellers

Grammar

1 Complete the shopping tips with verbs, articles or quantifiers where necessary. More than one option is possible in one case.

THE GREEN GUIDE

Shopping Tips: televisions

The days when ¹ _____ TVs came in only a ² _____ of types – colour or black and white – have gone. Today's flat screen TVs ³ _____ been developed to give ⁴ _____ best possible picture quality, with ⁵ _____ different viewing options that can ⁶ _____ set by the user.

Many people get ⁷ _____ new TV because they want ⁸ _____ bigger screen. However, bigger TVs use a lot of ⁹ _____ energy. A 52-inch LCD uses twice the power of a 32-inch model. Last year, new statistics ¹⁰ _____ published by the United States Department of Energy. They said the amount of ¹¹ _____ power that ¹² _____ used by TVs in America could supply electricity to all homes in ¹³ _____ state of New York for a year. One major factor in TV power use is the picture setting. ¹⁴ _____ people realize what a difference the settings can make. Electricity use ¹⁵ _____ be cut by up to 50 per cent if you change to ¹⁶ _____ efficient setting.

2 Read the shopping tips in Exercise 1 and find:
1. one positive and one negative thing about modern TVs.
2. one way of reducing the amount of energy your TV uses.

3 >> MB Work in pairs. Underline the five passive forms in the text in Exercise 1. Why are the passive forms used in the text?

4 >> MB Write sentences about some of the products and their raw materials. Use these verbs in the passive. Then work in pairs. Take turns to read your sentences without saying the subject. Try to complete your partner's sentences.

grow   import   make   manufacture   mine
produce

1. a bar of chocolate   cocoa beans   Ghana
2. a pair of jeans   cotton   Egypt
3. jewellery   gold   South Africa
4. perfume   flowers   France
5. mobile phone batteries   lithium   Chile
6. a loaf of bread   wheat   Canada

... have been grown in Ghana for many years.

I CAN	
use the passive	☐
use articles and quantifiers	☐

Vocabulary

5 Work in pairs. What could a shop assistant or customer say using each of these words?

delivery   exchange   gift-wrapping   in stock
receipt   return

6 >> MB Work in pairs. Take turns to give a definition or example of one of these things for your partner to identify.

budget   checkout   deals   goods   purchases
special offer   the sales   value for money

7 >> MB Work in pairs. Take turns to choose one of the shops in the photos. Your partner has 30 seconds to name six things you can buy there.

I CAN	
talk about shopping	☐
ask for and give product and sales information in a shop	☐
talk about everyday things we buy for ourselves and others	☐

Real life

8 Complete the questions and statements. Then write customer (C) or shop assistant (S).
1. We accept _____ by card or in cash.
2. Can I bring it _____ if I don't like it when I get home?
3. Let me see if this model is in _____ .
4. How much do you _____ for delivery?
5. Do you have the reference _____ ?
6. Can I have a _____ at this watch?
7. It's reduced – it's got 20 per cent _____ .
8. Excuse me, are you _____ this department?

9 >> MB Work in pairs. Take turns to be the customer and the assistant in a shop. Act out conversations in which you buy a tablet, a computer, a motorbike and some perfume.

I CAN	
buy and sell items in a shop	☐

Unit 10 No limits

On the annual *Marathon des Sables* in southern Morocco, keeping the sand out of your face can be a problem.

FEATURES

46 Leaving Earth

Could we live on another planet?

48 The superhumans

Find out about the latest advances in medicine

50 Two journeys, two lives

Read about two people who have endured tough experiences

54 What does an astronaut dream about?

A video about the first British woman in space

1 Work in pairs. Look at the photo and the caption. What other problems do you think runners like this face?

2 ▶ 80 Listen to an extract from a podcast about the *Marathon des Sables*. How many of your ideas from Exercise 1 are mentioned?

3 ▶ 80 Listen to the extract again and make notes about these things. Does ultrarunning appeal to you? Why? / Why not?

1 the age of the runners
2 the distances
3 anything else that interested you

4 Work in groups. Discuss the questions.

1 Other extreme sports include bungee jumping, BASE jumping, cave diving and free climbing. Have you tried any of them?
2 Why do you think people push their bodies to the limit?
3 Can you think of any dangers in pushing your body to extremes?

my life ▶ I'D LOVE TO LIVE IN … ▶ HEALTH EXPERIENCES ▶ INSPIRATIONAL PEOPLE ▶ TALKING ABOUT INJURIES
▶ A PERSONAL EMAIL

45

10a Leaving Earth

Reading

1 Work in pairs. Discuss the questions.

1 Do you think the human race will ever be able to live on another planet?
2 What kind of thing might make life on another planet difficult for humans?

2 Read the article. Answer the questions.

1 Which planets does the article mention?
2 Where are the planets?
3 Which planet do scientists already know something about?
4 Why is the colour blue important when looking at planets?

LEAVING EARTH

▶ 81

Professor Stephen Hawking has said that the human race has no future if it doesn't go into space. The planet we currently know most about is Mars. Two crewless spacecraft have already landed on the surface and have sent a lot of information to scientists on Earth.

But if we sent astronauts to Mars, would they be able to survive? How easy would it be to set up a base? We already know there would be some difficult challenges to face. Communication with Earth would have a 20-minute delay, food and water would only be provided every few months and astronauts couldn't go outside the base if they didn't wear a spacesuit. It all sounds more like science fiction than something that might actually happen.

Meanwhile, astronomers are searching for Earth-like planets outside our solar system. They hope to take images of planets in Alpha Centauri, the closest star system to Earth. According to Chris Lintott, an astrophysicist at Oxford University, it would be hugely exciting if we could get images from Alpha Centauri. If we had only a tiny image, astronomers could work out the planet's orbit and its size and colour. If the planet turned out to be blue, this might mean it had water and an atmosphere – and where there's water, there's life.

Of course, getting to such a distant planet is a different question – it makes a trip to Mars sound easy by comparison.

crewless (adj) /ˈkruːləs/ without any people – crew – working on board

46

3 Work in groups. Do you agree with these online comments about space exploration? Give your reasons.

1 'We can't look after Earth, so we'll never be successful on another planet.'
2 'I don't understand why we need to go into space. We should spend the money on improving life on Earth.'

Grammar **second conditional**

> **SECOND CONDITONAL**

But **if we sent** astronauts to Mars, **would they be able to** survive?
Astronauts **couldn't go** outside the base if they **didn't wear** a spacesuit.
It **would be** hugely exciting **if we could get** images from Alpha Centauri.
If the planet **turned out** to be blue, this **might mean** it had water.

For further information and practice, see page 90.

4 Look at the grammar box. Answer the questions.

1 Which verb form follows *if* in the second conditional?
2 When is a comma used in a second conditional sentence?
3 Which three verbs are used before the infinitive without *to* in the main clause?

5 Look at how the second conditional patterns are used in the article. Answer the questions.

1 Does the second conditional refer to situations in the past or in the present and the future?
2 Does the second conditional refer to real or to unreal situations?

6 Complete the comments about space exploration with the second conditional.

1 I _____ (consider) training as an astronaut if I _____ (have) the right qualifications.
2 I _____ (pay) to be a space tourist if it _____ (not / be) so expensive.
3 Being in space _____ (be) OK if you _____ (be able) to have Skype chats with people outside.
4 If we _____ (find) Earth-like planets, we _____ (not / be able) to travel there.
5 If I _____ (be) on a long space journey, I _____ (miss) my family.
6 What _____ (happen) if you _____ (not / get on) well with the rest of the crew on a spacecraft?
7 If you _____ (be) in charge of NASA, what _____ you _____ (spend) money on?
8 If there _____ (be) life on another planet, they _____ (contact) us first?

7 Work in pairs. Look again at the comments in Exercise 6. Say which statements (1–5) you agree with and answer the questions (6–8).

8 Complete the sentences with endings that are true for you. Then work in pairs and compare your sentences.

1 If I was a tourist on a space trip,
a I'd …
b I wouldn't …
c I could …
d I might …
2 If I lived on a base on Mars as part of the first exploration,
a I'd …
b I wouldn't …
c I could …
d I might …

9 Work in two pairs within a group of four. Play a guessing game.

Pair A: Turn to page 81 and follow the instructions.

Pair B: Turn to page 82 and follow the instructions.

Speaking my life

10 Work on your own. Think of a place you'd like to live in. Note down five reasons why you'd like to live there. Then work in groups. Take turns to tell your group the reasons, but don't say the place. Can they guess before you give all the reasons?

A: I'd love to live in beep. I**'d go** to all the local football matches.
B: And if I **lived** in bzzz, I'd never **be** cold again.

11 Think about your answers to these questions. Then tell the class.

1 If you could start a new life, what things would you change and how?
2 What would you miss about your 'old' life?

10b The superhumans

Listening

1 Work in pairs. Look at the photo. What do you think it shows?

2 ▶ 82 Listen to a preview of a TV programme. Tick the topics you hear mentioned.

> blades
> extreme sports
> Olympic medals
> Paralympic athletes
> progress in medical science
> wheelchairs

3 ▶ 82 Match the beginnings of the sentences (1–7) with the endings (a–g). Then listen again and check.

1 The Paralympics is a sports event for people
2 The TV programme features some athletes
3 A bionic device is one
4 Amanda Boxtel uses a robotic structure
5 The structure
6 Amanda Boxtel works with an organization
7 There's no limit to the things

a whose devices are bionic.
b which supports her body.
c bionic devices will be able to do.
d that promotes bionic technology.
e that uses electronics.
f who have a disability.
g Amanda Boxtel uses is called an exo-skeleton.

4 How do you think life might be different for someone with a bionic device compared to a traditional device? Tell your partner.

Grammar defining relative clauses

> ▶ **DEFINING RELATIVE CLAUSES**
>
> **With relative pronouns**
> 1 Tonight, there's **a documentary which features** some famous Paralympians.
>
> **With optional who/that/which**
> 2 **The Paralympians (who/that) you mentioned** use blades and wheelchairs.
> 3 **The range of devices (which/that) the programme describes** is growing.
>
> For further information and practice, see page 90.

5 Look at the grammar box. Choose the correct option.

1 In sentence 1, a documentary is the *subject / object* of the verb *features*.
2 In sentence 2, *the Paralympians* is the *subject / object* of the verb *mentioned*.
3 In sentence 3, *the range of devices* is the *subject / object* of the verb *describes*.
4 When *who, that* or *which* refers to the *subject / object*, we can miss it out.
5 We can use *that* instead of *who / which / both who and which*.

6 Look at the sentences in Exercise 3. Find the two types of clauses. Add a relative pronoun to the sentences that don't have them.

7 Look at the diagram of a bionic body. Complete the information for each numbered part with the words in the box. Use two words twice.

| when | where | who | which | whose |

1 implants in the ears .... allow people .... are deaf to hear
2 prosthetic arms .... can receive signals from the brain
3 temporary artificial hearts for people .... are waiting for transplants
4 the first replacement hips – from a time .... bionics was an idea from science fiction
5 healthy area of bone .... the bionic limb is attached
6 bionic limbs .... movement mimics the body's natural steps

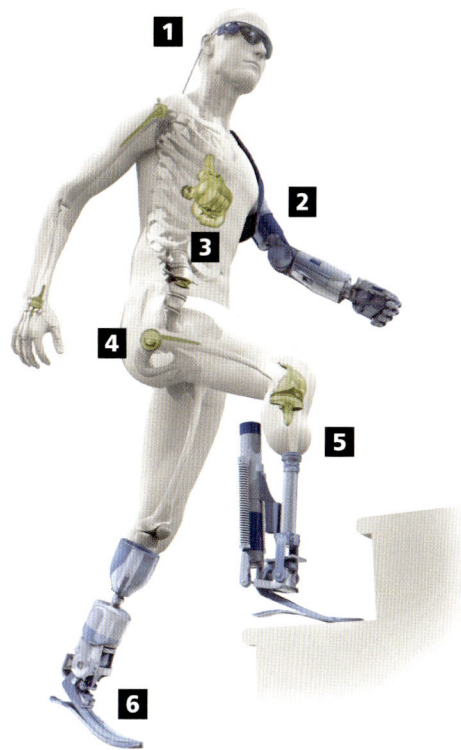

8 Read the comments from a hospital patient. Write *who, which* or *that* in the correct optional place.

1 The doctor I spoke to was very positive.
2 I thought the treatment I got was very good.
3 The injections the nurse gave me didn't hurt much.
4 The other patients I met had similar injuries.
5 The hospital ward I was in had only one other patient.
6 I didn't like the food they served us.

9 ▶83 Cross out any optional words in these sentences. Then listen and check your answers.

1 I know someone who has a bionic arm.
2 The hospital that we go to isn't far away.
3 Cochlear implants are devices that improve hearing.
4 I think people who do Paralympic sports are amazing.
5 Wheelchairs are often used by patients whose legs are paralyzed.
6 The doctor who we saw in the film is a pioneer in bionics.

10 Pronunciation sentence stress

a ▶83 Listen to the sentences from Exercise 9 again. Notice how the relative pronouns are not stressed.

b ▶83 Listen again and repeat the sentences.

Vocabulary medicine

11 Work in pairs. Choose the best option.

1 Several people were *injured / wounded* in the accident.
2 It's just a small cut. It will *treat / heal* naturally.
3 What time is your doctor's *appointment / date*?
4 They can't *cure / heal* this yet, but they can relieve the symptoms.
5 Where does it *hurt / pain*?
6 The *healing / treatment* has some unpleasant side effects.
7 The doctor is *controlling / monitoring* the patient's condition.
8 The injection isn't *hurtful / painful*.

12 Work in groups. Take turns to choose a word and then give a definition of the word.

*Botox is something **which** celebrities use to make themselves look younger.*

surgeon **injection**
botox **operating theatre** **blood test**
A & E (accident and emergency)
scan **ambulance** **stitches**
donor **crutches**
surgery **radiographer** **ward**
X-ray **paramedic** **first aid**

Speaking my life

13 Choose two of the words from Exercise 12 and talk about your own experience.

I've never been in an ambulance.

my life ▶ I'D LOVE TO LIVE IN … ▶ HEALTH EXPERIENCES ▶ INSPIRATIONAL PEOPLE ▶ TALKING ABOUT INJURIES
▶ A PERSONAL EMAIL

49

10c Two journeys, two lives

Reading

1 How much do you know about these people? Choose the option (a–c) you think links them.

a They broke 'unbreakable' records.
b They were successful in spite of difficulties.
c They became rich and famous in their chosen careers.

> J. K. Rowling
> Marie Curie
> Nelson Mandela
> Stephen Hawking

2 Work in pairs. You are going to read about two people who overcame obstacles in their lives.

Student A: Read about Diane Van Deren.

Student B: Read about John Dau.

Make notes to answer these questions.

1 Who?
2 Where?
3 When?
4 Distance covered?
5 Time taken?
6 Food and drink?

3 Tell your partner about the story you read. Use your notes to help you. Ask your partner at least one question about their story.

4 Now read your partner's story. Is the story what you expected to read? Did anything surprise you?

Word focus *take*

5 Look at these extracts from the stories. What do the expressions with *take* mean or refer to? Choose the correct option (a–c).

1 Diane Van Deren was […] **taking part** in the Yukon Arctic Ultra.
   a leaving   b participating   c winning
2 Van Deren […] had a kiwi-size piece of her brain **taken out**.
   a removed   b repaired   c returned
3 […] a journey which had **taken** him **more than half of his life**.
   a distance   b speed   c time
4 Dau […] **took care of** a group of younger children.
   a controlled   b looked after   c played

6 Work in pairs. What do the expressions with *take* mean in these sentences?

1 The Yukon Arctic Ultra **takes place** every two years.
2 Diane Van Deren **took up** running after an operation to cure her epilepsy.
3 Diane Van Deren couldn't **take off** her boots because they had frozen to her feet.
4 John Dau's plane to New York **took off** from Nairobi airport.
5 The fighting in Sudan **took away** John Dau's childhood.
6 John Dau **took up** a scholarship to study in the United States.

7 Using the information in the stories and your own understanding of them, discuss the questions with your partner.

1 Why did Diane Van Deren and John Dau begin their journeys?
2 Did they make their journeys through choice or necessity?
3 What have they achieved for themselves as a result of their journeys?
4 What have they achieved for others as a result of their journeys?

Critical thinking reading between the lines

8 Read the quotes. Who do you think said each one – Diane Van Deren or John Dau? Give your reasons.

1 'I think people refuse to try things because they fear failure.'
2 'All I have to think about is my body.'
3 'There have been many impossible situations in my life, but I keep trying.'
4 'You can't give up.'

9 Do you know of other people who have overcome obstacles to achieve something in unexpected ways?

Speaking my life

10 You are going to nominate an inspirational person for a prize. Choose someone from one of these categories. Make short biographical notes about the person and the reasons why you find them inspirational. Then give your presentation.

- art, music and fashion
- business and academia
- film and television
- local life
- science and medicine
- sport and adventure
- technology

Diane Van Deren

▶ 84

ON 15 FEBRUARY 2009, DIANE VAN DEREN WAS ONE OF A DOZEN RUNNERS TAKING PART IN THE YUKON ARCTIC ULTRA, A 700-KILOMETRE RACE ACROSS THE FROZEN ARCTIC IN THE MIDDLE OF WINTER. Not a single woman
5   had ever completed it. With temperatures of 30 degrees below zero and only seven hours of daylight each day, it's probably the hardest race in the world. But then, there is no woman like Diane Van Deren.

Twelve years earlier, Van Deren, a former professional
10 tennis player, had a kiwi-size piece of her brain taken out. It was part of the treatment for the epilepsy which she suffered from. The operation was successful, but she noticed one unexpected result: she could run without stopping for hours.

15 At the start of the Arctic Ultra, icy winds froze Van Deren's water supplies so she had nothing to drink for the first 160 kilometres. She kept going by sucking on frozen fruit and nut bars. On the eleventh day, the ice beneath her feet cracked open and Van Deren fell up
20 to her shoulders into a freezing river. She managed to climb out, but it was hard to continue. Her boots had frozen to her feet.

Yet somehow through it all, Van Deren remained positive. This was perhaps helped by another curious result of her operation. 'I have a problem with   25
short-term memory. I could be out running for two weeks, but if someone told me it was day one of a race,' she jokes, 'I'd say, "Great, let's get started!"'

On 26 February 2009 – exactly twelve years after her surgery – Van Deren crossed the finish line of the Arctic   30
Ultra. She was one of eight people who finished – and the first and only woman.

---

epilepsy (n) /ˈepɪˌlepsi/ an illness affecting the brain

John Dau

▶ 85

IN 2001, JOHN DAU BOARDED A PLANE TO NEW YORK. IT WAS THE BEGINNING OF ONE TRIP BUT THE END OF A JOURNEY WHICH HAD TAKEN HIM MORE THAN HALF OF HIS LIFE. In 1987, aged thirteen, Dau had run away from
5   his home in southern Sudan, escaping from the soldiers who came to destroy his village. He met up with a small group of boys like himself and together they walked for weeks to reach a refugee camp in Ethiopia. 'I had no shoes and no clothes; at night the desert was so cold.
10 We thought about our parents all the time,' remembers Dau. The boys had no food and nothing to drink. 'We chewed grass and ate mud to stay alive.'

The boys walked by night and slept by day. Eventually they reached the camp, where Dau spent the next
15 four years. As one of the older boys, Dau led and took care of a group of younger children which eventually numbered 1,200. But Dau was forced to run again when soldiers came to the camp. Along with 27,000 other boys, he set off to walk back to Sudan. To get there
20 they had to cross Gilo River. 'Soldiers were shooting at us, so we had to dive into water full of crocodiles,' Dau recounts. Thousands of boys were killed or caught and

only 18,000 of them arrived in Sudan. But the area was soon attacked again, so Dau and the other 'Lost Boys' of Sudan set off south again, this time to a camp in Kenya.   25
By now, Dau had walked more than 1,600 kilometres.

Ten years later, Dau was one of a handful of 'Lost Boys' who were sponsored to study in the USA. A new kind of journey was about to begin.

---

refugee camp (n) /ˌrefjʊˈdʒiː kæmp/ a temporary home for people who have left their country of origin

---

my life ▶ I'D LOVE TO LIVE IN … ▶ HEALTH EXPERIENCES ▶ **INSPIRATIONAL PEOPLE** ▶ TALKING ABOUT INJURIES
▶ A PERSONAL EMAIL

51

10d First aid

Vocabulary injuries

1 Work in pairs. Complete the table with the things that cause these injuries. Some things can cause more than one injury. Add at least one more cause of each injury.

Cuts and bruises	Sprains and breaks	Allergic reactions

blades and knives
falling off something
falling over
food poisoning
insect bites
tripping up
wasp and bee stings

2 For each injury, decide with your partner what is the best thing to do.

Real life talking about injuries

3 ▶86 Look at the expressions for describing injuries. Which expressions refer to the injuries in Exercise 1? Then listen to three conversations and check.

> ▶ **TALKING ABOUT INJURIES**
>
> **Describing injuries**
> I feel a bit sick.
> I've been stung.
> It doesn't hurt.
> It hurts when I move it.
> It looks a bit swollen.
> It might need stitches.
> it's just a sprain.
> It's painful.
> That looks nasty!
> You might have broken something.
> It's nothing.
>
> **Giving advice**
> If I were you, I'd go down to A and E.
> I would keep an eye on it.
> I wouldn't just ignore it.
> You should put some antihistamine cream on it.
> You'd better wash it straightaway.
> Why don't you go and see Rosana?
> It might be worth getting it X-rayed.
> It's probably best to get it looked at.
> Have you tried putting cream on it?

4 ▶86 Listen to the conversations again. What advice is given in each case? Check your answers in the expressions for giving advice.

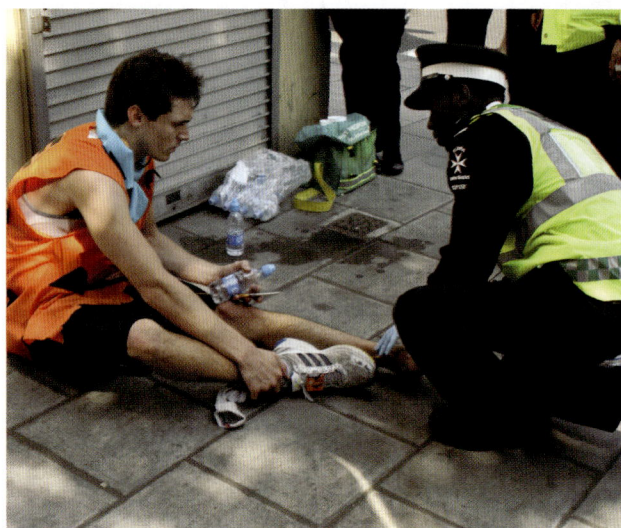

5 Pronunciation *and*

a ▶87 Listen to these expressions. Notice how *and* is not stressed.

A and E	wasp and bee stings
cuts and bruises	bites and stuff
sprains and breaks	go and see Rosana

b ▶87 Listen to the expressions again. Notice how *and* is linked to the word before it and how the *d* isn't pronounced. Repeat the expressions.

c Match words from A with words from B. Practise saying the pairs of words.

A day   doctors   eyes   food   fruit   hands
mind   rich

B body   drink   ears   famous   knees
night   nurses   nuts

6 Work as a class. You will be assigned a role as a patient or a doctor.

Patients: Choose one of the injuries from the list and think about how you will describe it to the doctor. Then visit each doctor and describe your problem. Who gives the best advice?

Doctors: Look at the list of injuries and think about appropriate treatment. Then listen to each patient and give advice. Which is the most difficult case to treat?

- a deep cut on your thumb from a kitchen knife
- a painful ankle after jumping off a trampoline
- feeling sick after being stung by a wasp
- multiple cuts and bruises after a mountain biking accident
- strange skin rash after a meal out
- neck and shoulder pain after a horse-riding accident

10e What do you think?

Writing a personal email

1 Who do you talk to when you need advice about these things? Work in pairs. Compare your ideas.

> car trouble   personal problems
> difficulties at work/school   relationship dilemmas
> health worries

2 Read the email. What is its purpose? Choose the best option (a–c).

a The writer is asking for information about a job opportunity.
b The writer is getting in touch with an old friend.
c The writer needs some help making a decision.

> Hi there,
>
> Thanks so much for the get well card! I'm feeling a lot better now, **actually**. And I've been meaning to write to you for a while – I want your advice about something.
>
> I've got the chance to spend a year away, on a project in the South Pacific. (I know, it sounds like paradise – I bet you wish you were me!) It's a job in a community health centre on Vanuatu. I'd have to do some training if I took the post, **of course**. I can do basic first aid, but I'd need to know more than that.
>
> **The thing is**, I'm not sure if I should go. It would mean giving up the job I've got now, **obviously**. But I wouldn't mind that – it's not a great job! And I've often thought about a career in nursing …
>
> **So**, what do you think?
>
> Hope all is well with you. **By the way**, did you manage to sell your car?
>
> Take care
>
> Kate

3 Is the style of the email formal, neutral or informal? Underline the words or expressions which show this.

4 What advice would you give to Kate? Tell your partner.

5 Writing skill linking ideas (2)

a Look at the table. Which group of words can replace each highlighted word or phrase in the email? Write the words from the email in the table. Add a comma where necessary.

1	clearly naturally	
2	in fact to be honest	
3	Before I forget, Incidentally,	
4	Anyway, Well,	
5	All the same, Even so, However,	

b Complete the sentences with expressions from Exercise 5a. Remember to add a comma where necessary. More than one answer is possible.

1 Your problem sounds familiar. I had to make a similar decision once, _____ .
2 It's a long way to go. You'd miss your family at first, _____ .
3 I hope I've helped you a bit! _____ how's your sister?
4 That's what I did. _____ I hope I've been of some help.
5 It could be interesting. _____ it's going to be difficult.

6 Think about a problem you need help with. Write an email to someone in your class.

7 Use these questions to check your email. Then send your email to the person you have chosen.

- Have you used a variety of linking expressions?
- Have you used linking expressions correctly?

8 Write a reply to the email you have received.

10f What does an astronaut dream about?

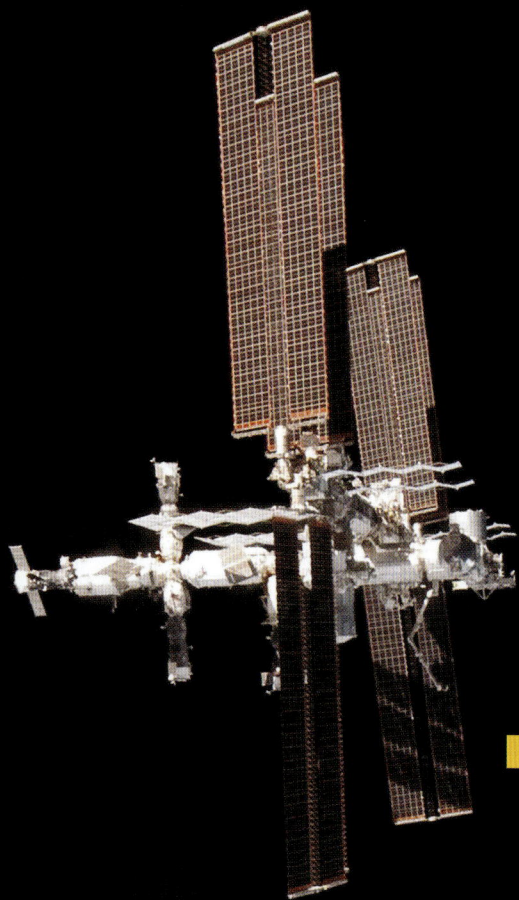

The Mir space station

Helen Sharman, the first British astronaut to go into space

Before you watch

1 Work in pairs. What do you think astronauts might dream about?

2 Key vocabulary

a Read the sentences. Try to guess the missing words.

1 In my job with an airline, it's important to have great _____ to work with.
2 Stones don't _____ on water, but pieces of wood usually do.
3 Since I left home, the thing I _____ most is my dad's cooking. He makes great pizza!
4 After six months travelling through China, we felt very _____ to the way of life there.
5 We'd read amazing reviews of the film, and when we saw it we weren't _____ . It was fantastic.

b Read the words in bold and their definitions. The words are used in the video. Complete the sentences in Exercise 2a with the words.

   a **float** (v) to move slowly on the surface of water or in air
   b **crewmates** (n) members of a team on a ship, plane or spacecraft
   c **miss** (v) to feel sad about things or people you aren't with now
   d **disappointed** (adj) to feel unhappy with something that wasn't as good as you'd hoped
   e **connected** (adj) linked or associated with a thing, place or person

3 Work in pairs. In the video you hear an astronaut, Helen Sharman, talking about being on the Mir space station. Can you guess how she uses the words in Exercise 2b?

While you watch

4 ▶10.1 Watch the video. In which order (1–3) does Helen Sharman talk about these things (a–c)?

   a her own feelings when she was on the Mir module
   b her dream
   c what astronauts feel when they look at Earth from space

5 ▶10.1 Watch the first part of the video (0.00–1.21) again. Choose the correct option.

1 She dreams about *the liftoff from Earth / being in space*.
2 She floats towards *a door / a window*.
3 She *sees / doesn't see* the stars.
4 Sergei and her other crewmates *are / aren't* in the dream.
5 She *looks out of / wants to leave through* the window.

6 ▶10.1 Watch the second part of the video (1.22–1.52). Complete the sentences with one word.

1 Everyone says the Earth looks _____ .
2 Helen Sharman felt disconnected and _____ to the Earth.
3 She knew it was her _____ .
4 She wanted to _____ .

7 Watch the third part of the video (1.53–2.27). Answer the questions.

1 Astronauts talk about different things at the start of a space trip and after a couple of days. What do they talk about?
2 What do they think about when they go over different countries?

8 ▶10.1 Work in pairs. How do you think Helen Sharman's dream ends? Watch the last part of the video (2.28 to the end) and check your ideas.

After you watch

9 Work in pairs. Compare your personal reactions to the video. Do you think the animation went well with Helen Sharman's words? Did anything surprise you? What was the overall message for you?

10 Vocabulary in context

a ▶10.2 Watch the clips from the video. Choose the correct meaning of the words and phrases.

b Complete the sentences in your own words. Then work in pairs and compare your sentences.

1 I only … on the odd occasion.
2 I never understand what … has to do with … .
3 If you asked me … , my response would be 'absolutely!'
4 On a cold night, it's nice to feel the warmth of … .
5 I was laughing and crying at once when … .
6 It's best to tell someone gently if … .

11 Work in small groups. Discuss the questions.

1 How often do you dream?
2 Do you usually have dreams or nightmares?
3 Do you remember your dreams?
4 Some people say dreams have meanings. Do you know of any common interpretations?
5 What do you think of the idea of interpreting dreams?

---

curvature (n) /ˈkɜːvətʃə/ the curve of the outline of the Earth seen from space
module (n) /ˈmɒdʒuːl/ a section of the space station
orientation (n) /ˌɔːrienteɪˈʃən/ the direction or way something is pointing
physical geography (n) /ˌfɪzɪkəl dʒiˈɒɡrəfi/ features such as mountains, rivers, deserts, etc.
rate (n) /reɪt/ speed
sedate (adj) /səˈdeɪt/ slow and unhurried

UNIT 10 REVIEW AND MEMORY BOOSTER

Grammar

1 Look at the photo of BASE jumping. Complete the comments about the activity with the second conditional.

1 You _____ absolutely terrified if it _____ the first time you did this. (feel / be)
2 If I _____ to the top of the cliff, I definitely _____ off. (get / jump)
3 If you _____ the last person left on the cliff top, _____ you _____ and go back? (be / turn around)
4 I _____ do this if you _____ me there. (not be able to / take)
5 You _____ yourself if something _____ wrong. (can kill / go)
6 If I _____ over the edge, I _____ sick. (look / feel)

2 Read the comments again. Which ones do you agree with?

3 ≫ MB Work in pairs. For each of these things, agree on a definition and an example. Then compare with another pair.

1 an adrenalin junkie
2 bravery
3 a dangerous place
4 extreme sports
5 a life-threatening situation

I CAN	
talk about improbable situations in the present or the future (second conditional)	
give descriptions or definitions of things which include essential information (defining relative clauses)	

4 ≫ MB Work in pairs. Discuss reasons for and against making BASE jumping illegal in the place in the photo. Use terms from Exercise 3. What's your conclusion?

Vocabulary

5 Complete the sentences with one word. The first letter is given.

1 This cut on my finger is taking ages to h_____ .
2 These machines m_____ the patient's condition.
3 The treatment is uncomfortable, but it's not p_____ .
4 Has she made an a_____ to see the doctor?
5 Ow, this bright sunlight h_____ my eyes!
6 Doctors t_____ several people for burns after the fire.

6 ≫ MB Work in pairs. Answer the questions in your own words.

1 How might you sprain your ankle?
2 What would you do if a bee stung you?
3 What kind of things are people allergic to?
4 Have you ever broken a bone?
5 Do you know anyone who is afraid of injections?
6 How serious is food poisoning?

I CAN	
talk about the body and injuries	
talk about medicine and emergency medical treatments	

Real life

7 Choose the correct option. Then decide what injury or illness each piece of advice could refer to.

1 You should *get / getting* an X-ray.
2 You'd better *phone / phoning* an ambulance.
3 It might be worth *go / going* to the doctor's.
4 Have you tried *take / taking* antihistamines?
5 If I were you, I'd *put / putting* some cream on it.

8 ≫ MB Work in pairs. Act out two conversations using advice from Exercise 7.

I CAN	
describe injuries and give first-aid advice	

Unit 11 Connections

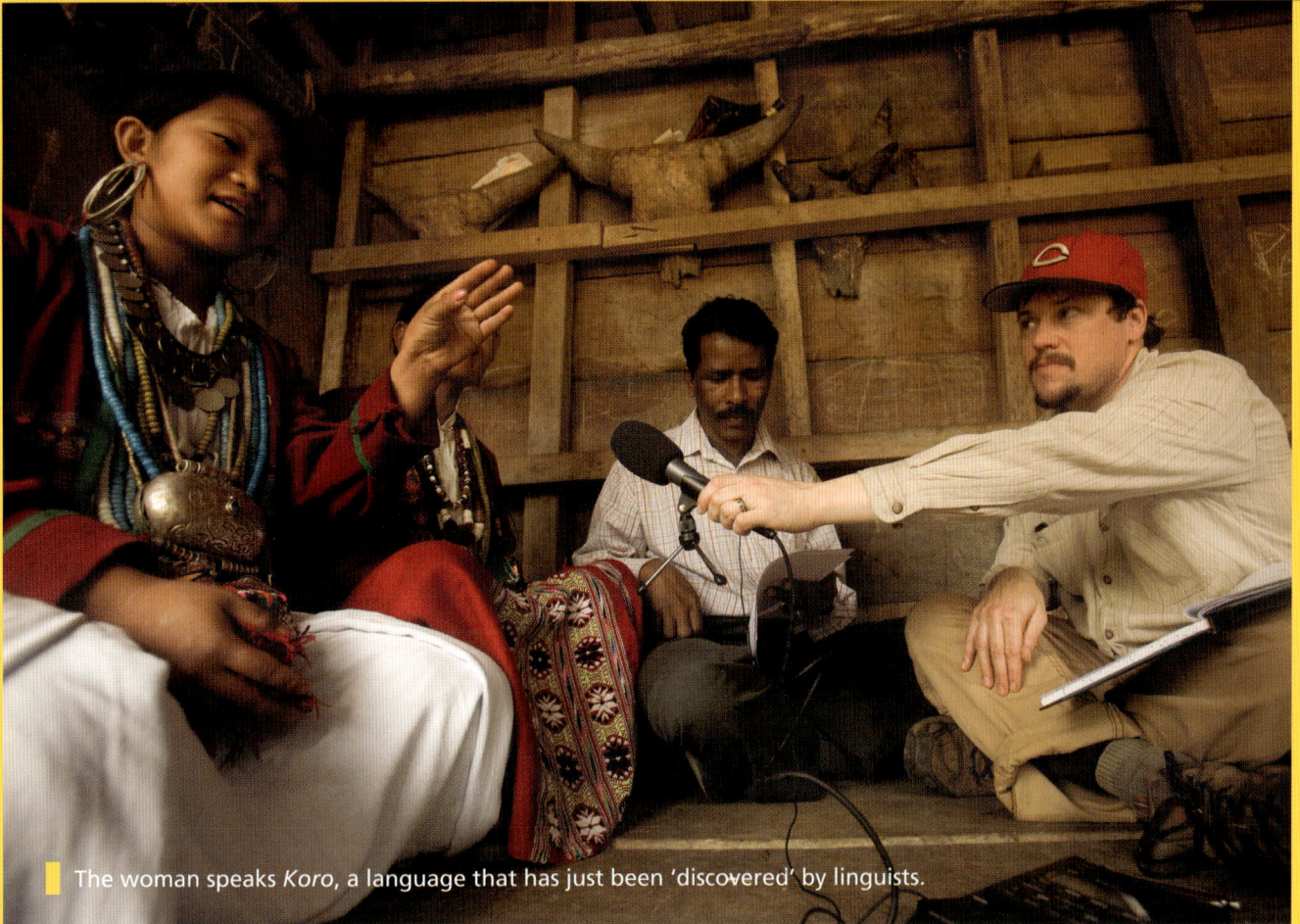

The woman speaks *Koro*, a language that has just been 'discovered' by linguists.

FEATURES

58 Uncontacted tribes

How a viral video revealed a controversial story

60 Sending a message

What's the best way to get your message across?

62 Spreading the news

An article about the impact of social networks

66 Can you read my lips?

A video about what it's like to have hearing difficulties

1 Look at the photo and the caption. Which of these parts of a news website do you think this photo would appear in?

business section	homepage
celebrity news	national news
comment and analysis	politics and society
current affairs	sports section
entertainment	technology
features	world news

2 Work in pairs. Read the comments about the news. Think of at least two ways to complete each comment.

1 'I get the headlines direct to my mobile so that …'
2 'I don't usually click on headlines unless …'
3 'I don't believe everything I read because …'
4 'I sometimes send a story to friends if …'

3 ▶ 88 Listen to four people answering questions about the news. Compare their comments with your ideas from Exercise 2.

4 Work in pairs. Look at the audioscript on page 100. Add two more questions to the four questions in the audioscript. Then work on your own and ask at least three other people your questions. Compare your results.

11a Uncontacted tribes

Reading

1 Work in groups. Look at the headline and the photo with the article. Discuss the questions.

1 What do you think the photo shows?
2 In which parts of the world would you expect to find uncontacted tribes?

2 Read the article. What kinds of organization are:

1 FUNAI?
2 *Survival*?
3 *Science*?

3 Find this information in the article.

1 what happened when the photos were published
2 what *Survival* and *Science* disagree about
3 who has had experience of contacting isolated tribes
4 who has collected information about isolated tribes for many years
5 what kind of life the Awá man had in the forest

4 Work in pairs. Read the Awá man's comments at the end of the article. Do you think he agrees with *Science* or with *Survival*? Give your reasons. Who do you agree with?

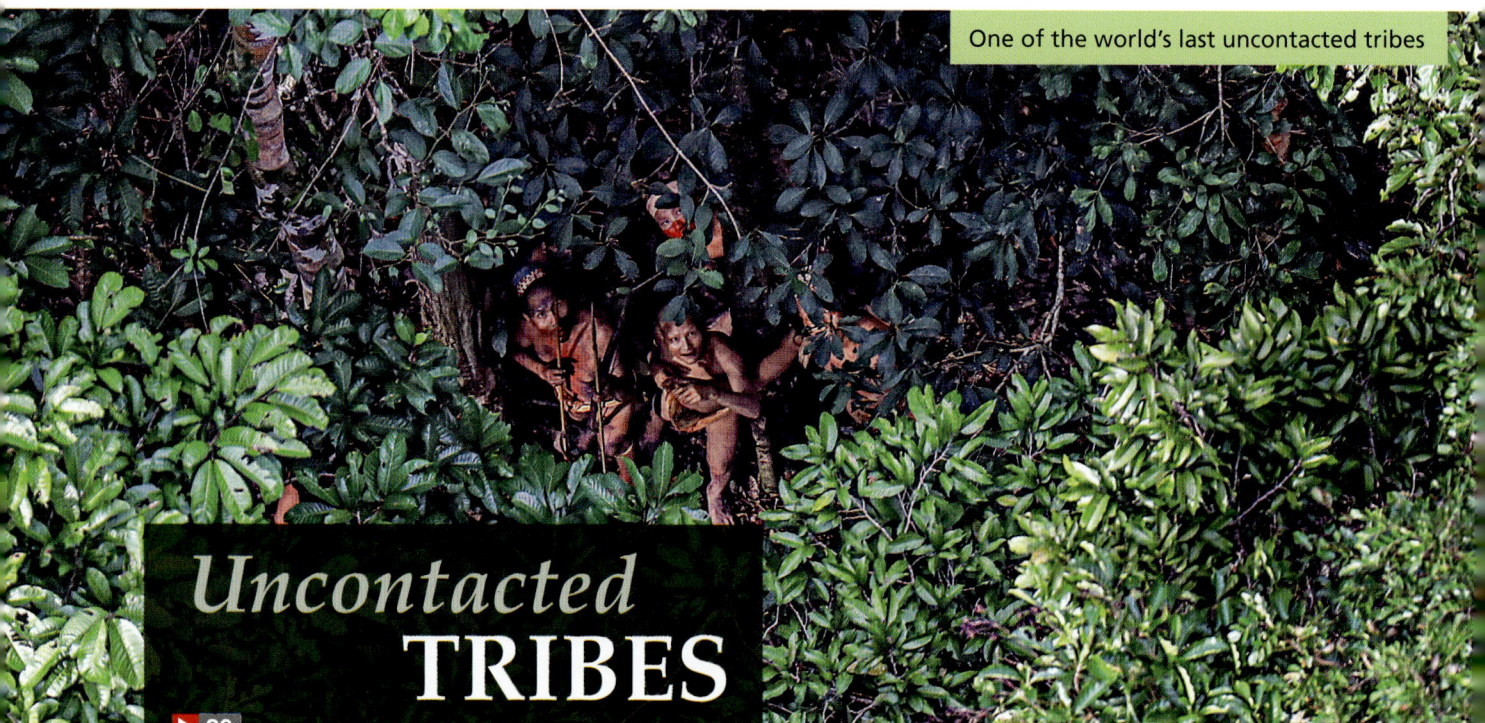

One of the world's last uncontacted tribes

Uncontacted TRIBES

▶ 89

Some years ago, the Brazilian department for Indian affairs (FUNAI) published photos of an uncontacted Amazonian tribe. FUNAI said that the tribe was under threat from exploitation of the Amazonian forest. Around the same time, a BBC documentary showed video of the same tribe. The photos went viral, leading to a reaction worldwide. Many online commentators asked what was being done to save the tribe. Some people also asked if contact with the outside world was actually a bad thing.

Several years after the viral video, the subject was still controversial. An article in the magazine *Science* said that it was possible to contact isolated Amazonian tribes safely. However, the NGO *Survival* disagreed. They quoted Sydney Possuelo, a former head of FUNAI who was talking about his experience with such tribes. He said that originally he had believed it would be possible to make safe contact and that he had organized one of the best prepared attempts at contact. He said at the

time that he wouldn't let a single Indian die. 'But,' he said, 'when the contact came, the diseases arrived, the Indians died.'

The authors of the article in *Science* said that isolated tribes aren't viable in the long term. However, FUNAI said that populations of the tribes they had been monitoring via satellite images had increased over a 30-year period.

Speaking to *Survival*, an Awá man from Brazil's north-eastern Amazon said that when he'd lived in the forest, he'd had a good life and that if he met one of the uncontacted tribes he'd say, 'There's nothing in the outside for you.'

---

exploitation (n) /ˌeksplɔɪˈteɪʃn/ the unfair use of someone for another person's benefit
isolated (adj) /ˈaɪsəˌleɪtɪd/ apart from others, alone
viable (adj) /ˈvaɪəbl/ able to be successful

Grammar reported speech

▶ REPORTED SPEECH

1 FUNAI **said (that)** the tribe **was** under threat.
2 He **said at the time (that) he wouldn't let** a single Indian die.
3 FUNAI **said** the populations **had increased** over a **30-year period.**
4 Commentators **asked what was being done** to save the tribe.
5 People **asked if** contact with the outside world **was** a bad thing.

For further information and practice, see page 92.

5 Look at the grammar box. Choose the actual words (direct speech) the people used. What has changed in the reported speech?

1 FUNAI said, 'The tribe *is / was* under threat.'
2 He said, 'I *won't let / wouldn't let* a single Indian die.'
3 FUNAI said, 'The populations *have increased / had increased* over the last 30 years.'
4 Commentators asked, 'What *is being done / was being done* to save the tribe?'
5 People asked, '*Is / Was* contact with the outside world a bad thing?'

6 Work in pairs. Find three more examples of reported speech in the article. Write them in direct speech.

7 Look at this sentence from the article. Choose the correct option.

The authors of the article in *Science* said that isolated tribes aren't viable in the long term.

When we report words that are still true at the time of reporting, we *need to / don't need to* change the verb form.

8 Write the direct speech as reported speech, changing the tenses correctly. Make changes to the pronouns and time expressions as necessary.

1 The BBC camerawoman said, 'I've been filming from a plane this morning.'
2 The BBC camerawoman said, 'We didn't speak to the people in the video.'
3 The FUNAI spokesman said, 'We'll publish the photos tomorrow.'
4 The FUNAI spokesman said, 'A million people have seen these photos in only three days.'
5 A viewer asked, 'How long did it take to make the film?'
6 Several viewers asked, 'Can I watch the video online?'
7 The BBC spokesman said, 'The film is being shown tonight.'
8 The interviewer asked, 'Will you go back again next year?'

9 Read about the first contact some tribes had with outsiders. Complete the text with the correct form of the verbs for reported speech.

In the *Survival* video *Stranger in the Forest*, tribal people of Brazil spoke of their experiences of first contact. One man said that his father [1] _____ (make) friends with three white men and then he [2] _____ (fell) ill. Another man explained that they [3] _____ (never have) contact with diseases like measles or malaria before – although there [4] _____ (be) diseases in the forest, they [5] _____ (not kill) people. He said a lot of useful knowledge about forest life [6] _____ (be) lost because older tribespeople [7] _____ (die). The final speaker said that his tribe [8] _____ (be suffering) as a result of contact with outsiders and asked the filmmakers how they [9] _____ (can stop) this happening.

Speaking and writing my life

10 You are going to act out a news item. Work in two pairs within a group of four.

Pair A: Turn to page 81 and follow the instructions.

Pair B: Turn to page 82 and follow the instructions.

11 Work in your group again. Act out the conversations. Then write a short news story about what happened to the other pair.

12 Compare your report with the original news item.

13 Work in pairs. Tell your partner about a viral photo or video you have seen.

11b Sending a message

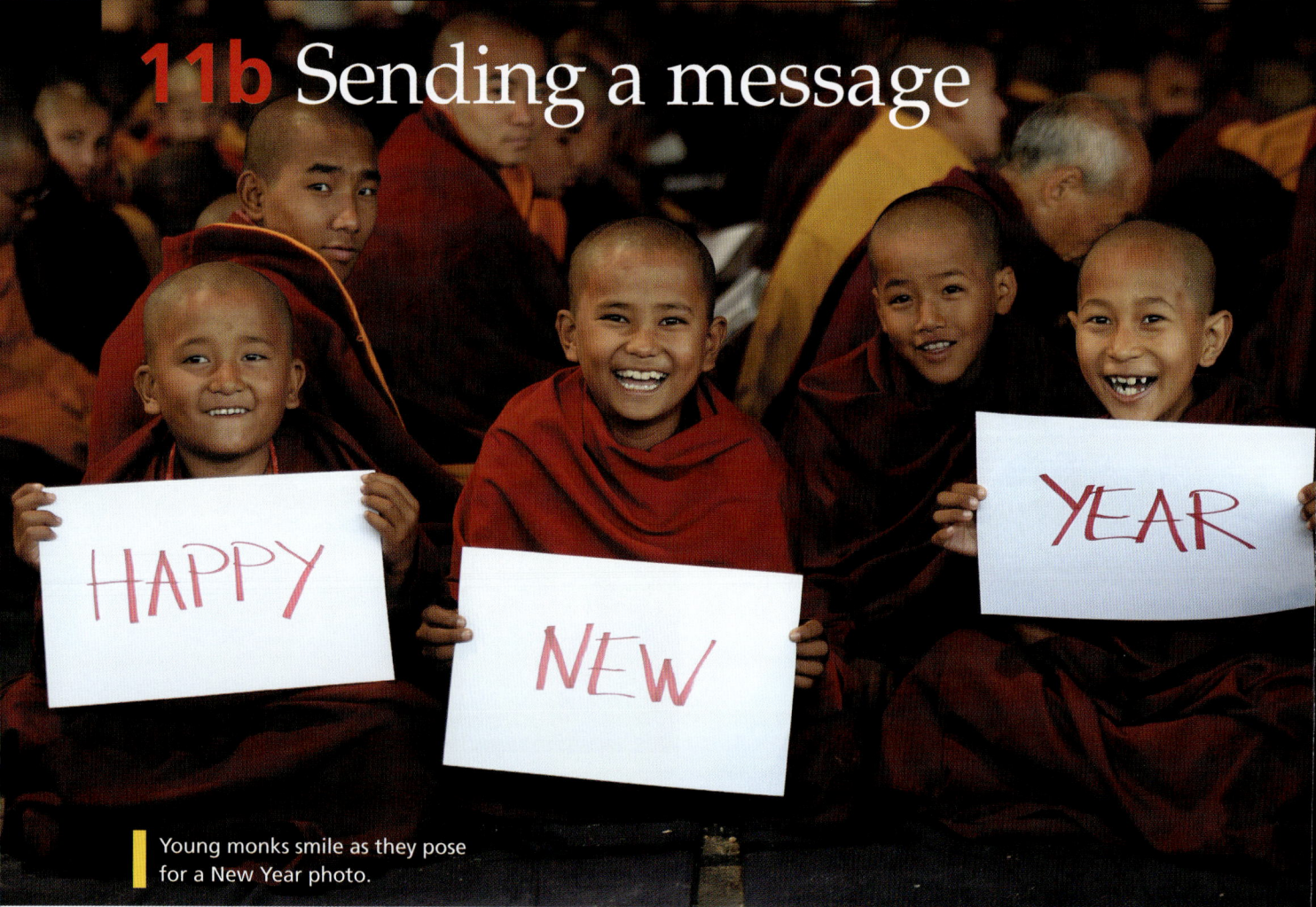

Young monks smile as they pose
for a New Year photo.

Vocabulary communications technology

1 Which of these things do you use?
Which apps or companies do you prefer
for each one?

instant messaging	blogs
search engines	social media
video messaging	

2 Work in pairs. Complete the questions in
your own words. Then ask and answer the
questions.

1 Do you follow anyone on _____ ?
2 Do you know how to upload videos to
_____ ?
3 Do you prefer calling or _____ your
friends?
4 Do you take many _____ ?

Listening

3 Work in pairs. Read the headlines. What do you think
the stories are about? Write one sentence for each
headline.

a Firm sacks workers by text

b YouTube or
'UFO-tube'?

c Email alert
warns of traffic
chaos

d How to enjoy
tomorrow's
eclipse of
the sun

e Tweet your way around the world

4 ▶ 90 Listen to four conversations about the headlines.
Write the number of the conversation next to the
headline. There is one extra headline.

5 ▶ 90 Listen to the conversations again. Choose the correct option (a–c).

1 The journalist asks her followers _____ .
   a to meet her for breakfast
   b to send in photos
   c to suggest things to do
2 The website reminds readers _____ .
   a not to bookmark the eclipse page
   b not to use telescopes
   c to check the weather
3 The company told people _____ .
   a not to turn up for work
   b not to use text messages
   c to come to work early on Monday
4 The politician has invited aliens _____ .
   a to come to his house
   b to come to a meeting
   c to watch his video

Grammar reporting verbs

> **REPORTING VERBS: PATTERNS**

ask / tell / remind / invite	someone	(not) to + infinitive
promise / offer		(not) to + infinitive

For further information and practice, see page 92.

6 Look at the grammar box. Then answer the questions.

1 Underline the reporting verbs in the sentences in Exercise 5. How many verbs are there?
2 What follows the reporting verbs in the sentences in Exercise 5 – a verb, a noun or the word *that*?
3 Which verb form is used for the reported words?

7 Write the actual words the people used for the sentences in Exercise 5. Sometimes, more than one answer is possible.

1 Can you suggest things to do?

8 Match the words in these sentences with the reporting verbs in the grammar box. Then write sentences reporting what the people said.

1 Dinah to Amy: 'Don't forget to turn off your mobile.'
   Dinah reminded Amy to turn off her mobile.
2 Jared to Dinah: 'Can you set up my email account?'
3 Amy to Jared: 'Come and watch the film on our new flat screen TV.'
4 Dinah to Amy: 'Plug in the battery charger first.'
5 Jared to Dinah: 'I can put those photos on the computer for you.'
6 Amy to Jared: 'Don't worry, I'll switch it off when I'm finished.'

9 Read the reported comments. Write the actual words the people used.

1 Dinah invited me to join her group online.
2 I asked Dinah to send me a link with the address.
3 I reminded Jared to sign out of his account.
4 Dinah offered to help me synchronize my email accounts.
5 I told Jared to delete the tweet.
6 Jared promised to upload the video for me.

> **REPORTING VERBS: THOUGHTS**

Verbs like *realize, think, know* and *wonder* have the same pattern as *say + that* and *ask + if/whether*.
*I **thought that** you **were coming** earlier.*
*Jared **wondered if/whether** you **had forgotten**.*

For further information and practice, see page 92.

10 Look at the audioscript on page 100. Underline reported thoughts with the verbs *realize, think, wonder* and *know*.

11 Pronunciation contrastive stress

a ▶ 91 Listen to these exchanges from two of the conversations in Exercise 4. Notice how the words in bold are stressed. Repeat the exchanges.

1 A: It's a great idea to use social media for something like that.
   B: I didn't realize social media could actually be useful for **anything**!
2 C: It says here there's an eclipse tomorrow. Did you know?
   D: Tomorrow? I thought it was **today**.

b ▶ 92 Listen to four other exchanges. Repeat the exchanges.

Speaking my life

12 Think of an offer, an invitation, a promise and a request for other people in the class. Write each one on a piece of paper. Make sure you include your name and the name of the other person.

from Francesca: I'll help Belinda upload her video.

13 Work in pairs. Exchange your pieces of paper. Then find the people and report what your partner said. Then report each person's reaction to your partner.

*A: Hi, Belinda. Francesca **has offered to help** you **upload** your video.*
B: Oh, great!

11c Spreading the news

Reading

1 Look at the photo and the caption. How many different things do you use your phone for?

2 Work in pairs. Are you familiar with these terms? What do you think they mean? Read the article quickly and underline the terms. Check your ideas.

internet access	community journalism
the digital divide	traditional media
media organizations	affordable technology

3 Read the article again. Find information about these things. Compare with your partner.

1 internet access in different places
2 mobile phone ownership in different places
3 *HablaGuate*
4 *CGNet Swara*

4 Answer the questions using information from the article.

1 What kind of technology is used by the community journalism projects described?
2 What kind of news stories don't usually appear in traditional news media?
3 What happens to the stories received by *CGNet Swara* before they are shared?
4 How successful is *CGNet Swara*?

5 Work in pairs. Find how these words are used in the article and decide if they are adjectives, nouns or verbs. Then try to think of another word that could replace them.

1 enables (line 27)   5 affairs (line 35)
2 links (line 28)   6 dial (line 44)
3 debate (line 29)   7 highlight (line 50)
4 rural (line 31)   8 issue (line 51)

6 Look at how the words in bold are used in these sentences. Which words in Exercise 5 have a similar meaning?

1 Living in a small **country** village, we are a long way from the city.
2 When you **call** the number, you hear a message.
3 Our class is going to **discuss** the main ideas of the film we watched today.
4 There are some serious environmental **problems** around the factory.
5 The motorway **connects** the two cities.
6 The news reports **emphasize** the fact that nobody was hurt in the accident.
7 There's a bus twice a day that **makes it possible for** us to get to school.
8 Following the expansion, everyone is hoping for an improvement in its financial **situation**.

7 Work in pairs. How is the community journalism described in the article different from traditional local journalism?

Critical thinking **opinions**

8 Look at the question in the title of the article again. Do you think the writer successfully answers this question?

9 Read these extracts from the article. The writer is expressing her opinion. Which words or phrases tell you this? What is her opinion in each case?

1 As a journalist myself, it seems clear that the digital divide is also a problem for media organizations.
2 Obviously, this has great benefits for rural communities.
3 Clearly, community journalism works.

10 Underline two places in the article where the author gives the opinion or view of other people. What two phrases does she use to introduce the opinion or view?

11 Which sentence (a–c) best summarizes the writer's view of the digital divide?

a The digital divide is a problem that needs to be solved as soon as possible.
b The digital divide doesn't exist any more, since so many people have mobile phones.
c The digital divide has resulted in successful alternative ways of connecting communities.

Speaking my life

12 Work in two pairs within a group of four. You are going to find out about new apps for mobile phones.

Pair A: Turn to page 81 and follow the instructions.

Pair B: Turn to page 82 and follow the instructions.

13 Tell the other students in your group about the most useful apps on your phone. Which one could you not live without?

SPREADING *the* *news*

Can we overcome the digital divide?

If these men in Kyrgyzstan had a signal, they could use their phones for more than just photos.

▶ 93

These days, the popular view is that we're all connected, all of the time, by the internet. But are we? On the one hand, we have people who live in cities. In many cities around the world, internet access is almost 100 per cent.
5 On the other hand, we have those who live in rural areas. Even in richer countries, the number of rural households with internet access is much lower than 100 per cent. And in some rural areas of India, for example, it's less than one per cent. This situation is what's known as the digital
10 divide – the gap between those who have and those who don't have the communications technology that gives them easy access to information. As a journalist myself, it seems clear that the digital divide is also a problem for media organizations.

15 Fortunately, the lack of internet access doesn't always mean that people can't connect to the wider world. That's because there is one type of technology that over three billion people do have access to – the mobile phone. And the great advantage of mobile phones is that you don't
20 need the internet to use them. Mobiles connect people to their friends and family, but they can also help to connect whole communities. In fact, a whole new type of community journalism can exist thanks to mobile phone technology.

Let's look at Guatemala – a country of fifteen million people
25 with twenty-two million registered mobiles. Guatemalan journalist Kara Andrade developed a project, *HablaGuate*, that enables people to send their stories to a community website from their mobiles. *HablaGuate* links communities, making it easier to debate and participate in the kind of local issues that don't usually make headlines in the
30 traditional media. Obviously, this has great benefits for rural communities. Following its success in Guatemala, Andrade has adapted the idea for other countries in Central America. As she says, affordable technology like mobiles enables people to become active in local affairs that affect their lives.
35

Halfway across the world, another journalist had a similar idea. Shubhranshu Choudhary used to report for the BBC in his home country, India. According to Choudhary, the best people to report on local issues are local people. He set up *CGNet Swara*, a current affairs network based around news
40 that is sent on mobiles. Since 2010, more than three hundred thousand stories have been sent to the network, of which about five thousand have been fact-checked and shared. To listen to the stories, users dial the number of the network and choose an option on a menu to hear audio clips. For example,
45 one story was from a man who reported that elephants were causing problems for his village. Another audio clip was from a woman who called in with the news that a local company had finally paid its workers the wages that they were owed. This was a direct result of her previous story that highlighted
50 the issue. What's more, the national media are now featuring some of the stories from *CGNet Swara.*

Clearly, community journalism works. And although the digital divide may be a problem for more traditional media organizations, some local communities have found ways of
55 overcoming this problem.

11d Can I take a message?

Real life telephone language

1 ▶ **94** Listen to two telephone calls. Note down the information.

1 Who is the call for?
2 Who is the call from?
3 What's the call about?

2 ▶ **94** Look at the expressions for telephone messages. Listen to the telephone calls again. Tick the expressions the speakers use.

> ▶ **TELEPHONE LANGUAGE**
>
> **Introductions**
> This is a message for Anna Price.
> Could I speak to Jess Parker, please?
> Is Jess there?
> Can I take a message?
> I wonder whether I could leave a message?
>
> **Message content**
> Can you ask her to ring me?
> It's about the apartment.
> I'm returning her call.
> I'd like to speak to her as soon as possible.
>
> **Caller's details**
> I'm on 96235601.
> My number is 96235601.
> Can I take your name, please?
> Who's calling?
>
> **Endings**
> I'll try and call you later.
> I'll phone back.
> I'll let her know that you rang.
> She'll get back to you.

---

3 ▶ **95** Listen to the conversations about the phone calls. Answer the questions.

1 Who is going to call Roger back?
2 How many messages does the secretary give Jess?

4 Pronunciation polite requests with *can* and *could*

a ▶ **96** Listen to four requests. Notice how the speaker's voice rises at the end in order to sound polite.

b Work in pairs. Practise making requests with *can* and *could* and these ideas. Pay attention to sounding polite.

1 give me your name / number / address
2 leave my name / number / address
3 ask him/her to call me back / get in touch / give me a ring
4 make an appointment
5 call round

5 Work in pairs. Look at the audioscript on page 100 for the second telephone call in Exercise 1. Take a role each and prepare your role. Then close your books and practise the conversation. Change roles and repeat the conversation.

6 Work in pairs. You are going to leave a message for someone in your class. Use the expressions for telephone messages to help you.

Student A: Choose a classmate (Student C). Decide what your message is. 'Phone' Student B and leave the message for Student C.

Student B: Take the message for Student C.

Then change roles and repeat the telephone call.

7 Work in a new pair with the classmate you took the message for. Give this person the message.

11e A point of view

Writing an opinion essay

1 Work in pairs. Look at the title of the essay. Discuss the question and make notes on at least two reasons to support your answer.

2 Read the essay and answer the questions.

1 Do you agree with the writer of the essay?
2 Does the essay include the ideas you had in Exercise 1?
3 What (other) ideas does the essay include?

DOES THE INTERNET MAKE IT EASIER FOR PEOPLE TO **KEEP IN TOUCH?**

1 These days, there are many different apps that allow you to communicate with other people. I think this makes it easier to stay in touch with friends and family, and also to make new friends.

2 Firstly, many people now have constant access to the internet via smartphones as well as tablets and PCs. This means that if you send someone a message, they will see it straightaway. I think that you stay in touch more easily when you can communicate quickly.

3 In addition, there are lots of different apps available. For example, you can share photos, videos and links with people as well as text messages. It's also very easy to have video chats. You can do all of these things either for a small charge or completely for free. Some people say it's not 'real' conversation, but I disagree. In my opinion, it's the same as writing letters used to be.

4 To sum up, I believe that the number of apps on the internet and the low cost make it very easy to keep in touch with people.

3 Writing skill essay structure

a Match the functions (a–d) with the paragraphs (1–4).

a additional opinions / other opinions / examples
b concluding statement referring to the ideas in the essay
c general statement and short response to the title
d statement to support your response

b Write the words and expressions from the essay that are used for these functions. Add a comma where necessary.

Starting a paragraph	....
Giving your opinion	....
Contrasting opinions	....
Giving examples	....

c Complete the essay with expressions from Exercise 3b. Remember to add a comma where necessary. More than one answer is sometimes possible. Compare with your partner.

1 _____ nearly everyone has a phone that lets them get online. I've read that experts think we spend too much time online and 2 _____ we sometimes feel pressure to answer messages quickly. But 3 _____ with both points.

4 _____ there are many great reasons to go online. 5 _____ you can use social media to connect with your friends. 6 _____ being online gives you access to lots of information.

7 _____ the advantages of being online outweigh the disadvantages.

4 Work in pairs. You're going to prepare an essay with four paragraphs. Choose one essay title. Write the introduction (paragraph 1) together. Look at your notes and decide which ideas can go together in paragraphs 2 and 3.

- Do people spend too much time online these days?
- Is it a good idea to have one day a week 'off' the internet?
- Do children under the age of ten need mobile phones?

5 Work on your own. Write paragraphs 2 and 3 to follow your introduction. Then write the concluding paragraph. Use expressions from Exercise 3b.

6 Use these questions to check your essay. Then exchange your essay with a new partner.

- Have you organized your essay correctly?
- Is your opinion clearly expressed?
- Have you used expressions from Exercise 3b correctly?

7 Work in pairs. Ask your new partner about one thing they wrote in their essay.

11f Can you read my lips?

Learning sign language at school

Before you watch

1 Work in groups. Why do people use these three things? How much do you know about them?

   1 a hearing aid
   2 sign language
   3 lip reading

2 Key vocabulary

a Read the sentences. The words in bold are used in the video. Guess the meaning of the words.

   1 We used to play the same games every **recess** when I was a kid.
   2 The art exhibition was also an **auditory** experience because each room had different music playing.
   3 This note from Jim isn't very **legible** – I can't work out what he's written.
   4 Some children **mumble** because they are too shy to speak loudly in front of a class.
   5 Some people don't accept the concept of climate change, although I don't think it's hard to **grasp**.
   6 We had to **wade** across a river, but luckily nobody fell in.

b Match the words in bold in Exercise 2a with these definitions.

   a describing sounds and hearing
   b a period of play between lessons at school (Am Eng)
   c to walk with difficulty through something wet
   d to understand something that seems difficult
   e words written clearly enough to be understood
   f to speak too quietly and not clearly enough to be understood

While you watch

3 ▶ **11.1** Watch the video. What is the woman, Rachel Kolb, saying at the end of the video?

4 ▶ **11.1** Work in pairs. Watch the first part of the video (00.00–01.10) again. Discuss what you think the video is demonstrating.

5 ▶ **11.1** Watch the second part of the video (01.11–02.22) again. Note down the things that can make lip reading difficult. Compare your answers with the class.

6 ▶ **11.1** Watch the final part of the video (02.23 to the end) again. Answer the questions.

   1 Does Rachel Kolb prefer to lip read or to sign?
   2 What does she say happens when lip reading works well for her?

After you watch

7 Work in pairs. What did you learn from this video?

8 Vocabulary in context

a ▶ **11.2** Watch the clips from the video. Choose the correct meaning of the words and phrases.

b Answer the questions in your own words. Then work in pairs and compare your answers.

   1 Can you remember a time when something clicked for you?
   2 How does it feel to launch into an explanation of something, then realize you don't really understand it?
   3 Being successful in life isn't a given. Do you agree with this statement?

9 ▶ **11.1** Work in small groups. Watch the section of the video from 02.58 to 03.10 again. What do you think the young woman is signing? Take turns to tell the group about something that has happened to you recently using only signs. How successful are you?

10 Look at the signs below. Practise spelling your name.

11 Work in pairs. Take turns to spell words for your partner to guess.

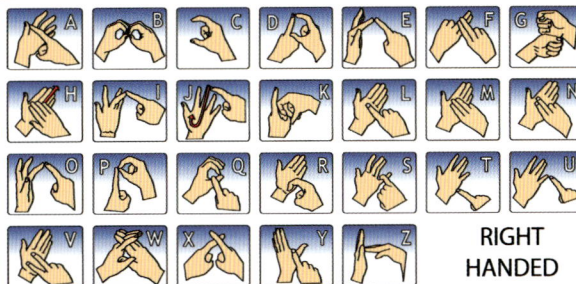

BRITISH SIGN LANGUAGE - **FINGERSPELLING**

RIGHT HANDED

british-sign.co.uk — LEARN BRITISH SIGN LANGUAGE ONLINE AT WWW.BRITISH-SIGN.CO.UK

grade (n) /greɪd/ a school year in the USA system
rely on (v) /rɪˈlaɪ ˌɒn/ depend on
swamp (n) /swɒmp/ an area of land that is a mixture of water, soil and plants

Grammar

1 Underline six reporting verbs in the news item. Write the words that were originally used.

Worries over lives lived online

The executive chairman of Google, Eric Schmidt, once said that there were only two states for children: 'asleep or online'. Recent studies claimed that vulnerable young people could become addicted to the online world and be unable to cope with the challenges of the real world. One study reported that teenagers who engaged with social media during the night could damage their sleep. The study said this would increase the risk of anxiety and depression in teenagers. Teenagers who tried 'switching off' for a week told researchers that they had enjoyed the break, but they were worried about conversations they had missed. Meanwhile, some organizations asked why the government wasn't looking at ways of educating young people more on this matter.

2 Read the news item again. Answer the questions.

1 What are the main risks associated with being online for young people?
2 How did some teenagers feel when they didn't go online for a week?

3 ⟫ MB Work in pairs. Tell your partner about three stories you have read or heard recently in the news. Say:

- where you read or heard the stories
- why you remember them
- what people involved in the stories said

I CAN	
report people's words (reported speech)	☐
use appropriate verbs to report people's words (reporting verbs)	☐

Vocabulary

4 Work in pairs. Give an example of the kind of story you would read about in these sections of a news website.

1	business section	5	national news
2	celebrity news	6	politics and society
3	entertainment	7	sports section
4	home page	8	world news

5 Match the beginnings of the sentences (1–4) with the endings (a–d)

1 I usually text
2 I've never followed
3 It's really easy to upload
4 My friend takes

a anyone on Twitter.
b my friends because it's quicker.
c photos of all her meals with her phone!
d videos these days.

6 ⟫ MB Work in pairs. What do you think are the most usual ways of staying in touch with these groups of people? Why?

cousins	immediate family
current friends	old school friends
ex-work colleagues	people you met on holiday
grandparents	

I CAN	
talk about news media	☐
talk about communications technology	☐

Real life

7 Work in pairs. Put the sentences from one half of a telephone conversation (a–e) into a logical order. Then act out the conversation, adding the other person's words.

a Thanks. I'll try and call him later, anyway.
b It's about the books he ordered. He asked me to ring him.
c OK. Well, could I leave a message?
d Yes, I'm on 548632 until about five this afternoon.
e Is Adam Meyer there, please?

I CAN	
leave, take and pass on telephone messages	☐

Sheep in the Scottish Hebrides islands

FEATURES

70 The man who ate his boots

Looking back at the mistakes of some British explorers

72 Experts in the wild

Listen to two stories about unexpected trouble

74 The legacy of the samurai

Find out about Japan's famous soldiers

78 Shark vs. octopus

A video about an encounter between a shark and an octopus

1 Work in groups. Look at the photo and the caption. What do you think the man's job is? What's he doing?

2 ▶ 97 Listen to an interview with a farmer from the Hebrides. Check your ideas from Exercise 1.

3 ▶ 97 Can you remember the answers to the interviewer's questions? Listen to the interview again and check.

1 Why do you need to move the sheep like this?
2 When do you bring them back?

4 Work in groups. Can you work out the solution to this farmer's problem?

A farmer has a fox, a chicken and a bag of grain. He needs to cross a river. He's got a boat, but he can only fit one other thing with him in the boat. Remember that foxes eat chickens and chickens eat grain. How does he get everything across the river?

12a The man who ate his boots

Reading

1 You are going to read a review of a book about Arctic expeditions called *The man who ate his boots.* Work in pairs. Discuss the questions.

1 What kind of environment is the Arctic region?
2 What might go wrong on an expedition to the Arctic?
3 How much do you know about the lifestyles of people who live in the Arctic?

2 Read the first paragraph of the book review. Find the following information.

1 the reason for the British expeditions
2 what happened to the expeditions in the end
3 two words to describe the British explorers

3 Read the whole review. Are these sentences true (T) or false (F)?

1 The British explorers learned a lot from the local Inuit people they met.
2 Tents were an appropriate type of shelter for Arctic conditions.
3 The British wore adequate clothing for the weather in the Arctic.
4 The British pulled their own sledges rather than use dog teams.
5 The British had no supply of vitamin C to treat scurvy.

4 What do you think the title of the book refers to? Tell your partner.

▶ 98

The man who ate his boots is a fascinating account of expeditions that went wrong. The book tells the story of the nineteenth century British search for a route to Asia via the Arctic (the Northwest Passage). Author Anthony Brandt describes many attempts by both land and sea that ended in failure and tragedy, including the 1845 expedition led by Sir John Franklin. Brandt shows how these brave, yet sometimes foolish, British explorers would have avoided starvation, frostbite and even death if they'd copied the survival techniques of the local Inuit people. Some of the more surprising details the book reveals include:

Tents
The British had seen how the Inuit built igloos, but they still used tents. Tents freeze in sub-zero temperatures and don't keep the people inside them warm. If the British had built igloos, they would have been warm even in the worst Arctic weather.

Clothing
Frostbite was common among the British but rare among the Inuit. If the explorers had worn sealskin and furs like the Inuit, they wouldn't have suffered from frostbite.

Dog teams
Why didn't the British use dog teams to pull their sledges? British explorers pulled their sledges themselves right into the early twentieth century. It cost Scott and his men their lives on their return from the South Pole in 1912.

Salad
The British did get something right, however, when Captain Edward Parry grew salad vegetables in boxes on board his ship. It was known that fresh vegetables and fresh meat prevented scurvy, although at that time the reason for this – not enough vitamin C – hadn't been discovered. Parry's men wouldn't have stayed healthy if they hadn't eaten the salads.

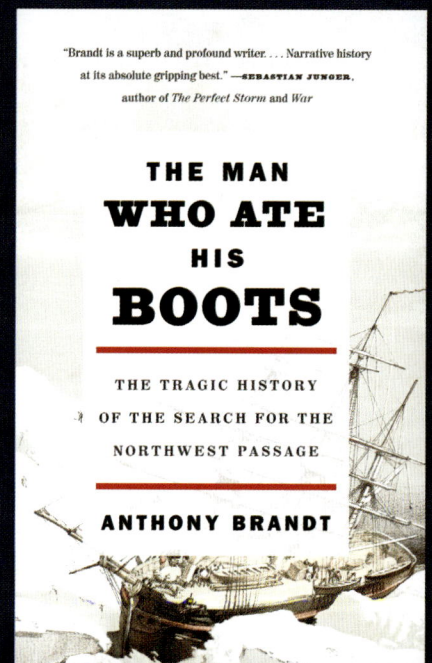

"Brandt is a superb and profound writer. . . . Narrative history at its absolute gripping best." —SEBASTIAN JUNGER, author of *The Perfect Storm* and *War*

THE MAN WHO ATE HIS BOOTS

THE TRAGIC HISTORY OF THE SEARCH FOR THE NORTHWEST PASSAGE

ANTHONY BRANDT

Read this amazing book and find out what these explorers had to do to survive.

frostbite (n) /ˈfrɒs(t)baɪt/ severe damage to the body caused by freezing conditions, usually affecting toes and fingers
scurvy (n) /ˈskɜːvi/ an illness affecting the mouth and teeth caused by lack of vitamin C
sledge (n) /sledʒ/ a wooden object for transporting people and things across snow
starvation (n) /stɑːˈveɪʃən/ death or loss of strength caused by not eating

Grammar third conditional

> **THIRD CONDITIONAL**
>
> 1 *If the British **had built** igloos, they **would have been** warm even in the worst Arctic weather.*
> 2 *Parry's men **wouldn't have stayed** healthy if they **hadn't eaten** the salads.*
>
> For further information and practice, see page 94.

5 Look at the grammar box. Which verb forms are used to make the third conditional?

6 Look at the grammar box again. Answer the questions.

    1 a Did the British learn to build igloos?
        b Were they warm in the worst Arctic weather?
    2 a Did Parry's men stay healthy?
        b Did they eat salads?

7 Find two more third conditional sentences in the book review.

8 Complete the sentences using the third conditional and the verbs in brackets.

    1 If the British _____ (wear) furs, they _____ (not / get) frostbite.
    2 The men _____ (not / be) exhausted if they _____ (use) dogs to pull their sledges.
    3 If the men _____ (take) essential items only, the sledges _____ (not / be) heavy.
    4 They _____ (not / become) ill if they _____ (know) their canned food was poisonous.
    5 One expedition _____ (not / get) stuck on the ice if they _____ (speak) to local people.
    6 If the expeditions _____ (follow) local customs, they _____ (be) successful.

9 Look at your completed sentences in Exercise 8. Say what actually happened.

    1 The British didn't wear furs. They got frostbite.

10 Work in pairs. Match the pairs of sentences. Then write a new sentence using the third conditional.

    1 We forgot to check our flight times.
       If we hadn't forgotten to check our flight times, we wouldn't have missed the plane.
    2 We didn't ask anyone for information.
    3 A local man gave us a map.
    4 We didn't plan things very well.
    5 The airline didn't let me take my bag on board.
    6 We didn't get into the museum for free.
    7 We didn't check the weather forecast.

    a I packed too much.
    b The holiday was a disaster.
    c We found our way to the castle.
    d We missed the plane.
    e We didn't take a phrase book.
    f We didn't take appropriate clothes.
    g We didn't have our student cards with us.

Speaking   my life

11 Think of three times in your life when you had to make a decision. They can be important or trivial decisions. Think about the answers to these questions.

    1 Was it easy or difficult to decide what to do?
    2 How did you decide?
    3 What would have happened if you had done something different?

12 Work in pairs. Tell your partner about your decisions. Ask your partner follow-up questions. Would you have done the same things?

    A: When we were in Year 10 at school, we had to choose which foreign language to study.
    B: Oh, so did we. What were your options?
    *A: French or German. And **if I'd chosen** German instead of French, …*

12b Experts in the wild

Listening

1 Work in pairs. Discuss the questions.

1 Have you ever been camping? If so, what did you take with you? What was the experience like?
2 If you haven't been camping, would you like to go? Give your reasons.

2 Read about Emma Stokes and Beth Shapiro. Answer the questions.

1 What do they do?
2 What kind of places have they travelled to?
3 What kind of things could cause problems in those areas?

Emma Stokes is a wildlife researcher who has led projects to protect gorillas and tigers. She often has to cut paths through the forest and set up a camp. Her first-ever expedition was to the Central African forest, where she had an unexpected experience.

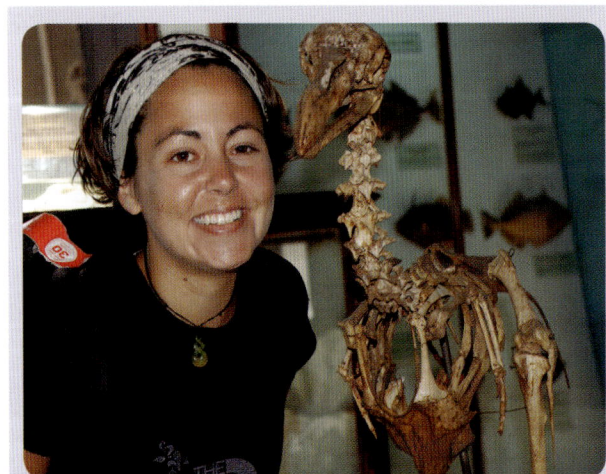

Beth Shapiro is a biologist and an expert on extinct mammal species. Much of her work is done on expeditions. She often goes to Siberia, where she hopes to find mammoth bones or tusks. On her first visit there, however, living animals caused the problem.

3 Work in pairs. You are going to listen to the stories of two difficult experiences Emma and Beth had. Before you listen, decide which story you think these words come from.

bones	mosquitoes
exhausted	remote
forest	rice
heavy steps	screaming

4 ▶ 99 Listen to the stories. Check your answers from Exercise 3.

mammoth (n) /ˈmæməθ/ an extinct animal, similar to an elephant
tracker (n) /ˈtrækə/ a person who shows you the way in a wild place
trumpeting (n) /ˈtrʌmpɪtɪŋ/ the noise made by elephants
tusks (n) /tʌsks/ two long teeth on the outside of the mouths of some animals

5 ▶ 99 Work in pairs. Look at the events from the two stories. Decide if they are about Emma (E) or Beth (B). Then listen to the stories again and put the events in order.

a She got her gear and got out of the tent.
b She had to take her mosquito net off her face to eat.
c She landed and set up camp.
d She was eaten alive by mosquitoes.
e The trackers woke her up by shouting.
f They made a meal of rice and fish.
g They made camp early one evening.
h When she went back, three of the tents were destroyed.

6 Work in pairs. What was the difficult experience in each case? What would you have done?

Grammar *should have* and *could have*

7 Read the comments. Who do you think said each one – Emma or Beth?

1 'We could have died.'
2 'We couldn't have avoided the insects.'
3 'We couldn't have imagined that would happen.'
4 'We should have checked the area before we camped.'
5 'We should have gone there at a different time of year.'
6 'We shouldn't have put up our tents there.'

8 Look at the sentences In Exercise 7 again. Match the sentences (1–6) with the meanings (a–d).

a This was the right thing to do, but we didn't do it.
b This was the wrong thing to do, but we did it.
c This was possible, but it didn't happen.
d This was impossible and it didn't happen.

▶ **SHOULD HAVE and COULD HAVE**

should (not) *could (not)*	*have* + past participle

For further information and practice, see page 94.

---

9 Look at the grammar box. Choose the best option to complete the sentences.

1 We *would / should* have brought more water – I'm really thirsty now.
2 The elephants came so close we almost *could / couldn't* have touched them.
3 We've run out of food – we *should / shouldn't* have known this would happen.
4 If I'd followed you, I *should / could* have got there more quickly.
5 I *should / would* have asked what was in the drink before I drank it.
6 If we'd taken the other road, we *wouldn't / shouldn't* have got lost.

10 Complete the story with *should (not) have, could (not) have* and past participle forms.

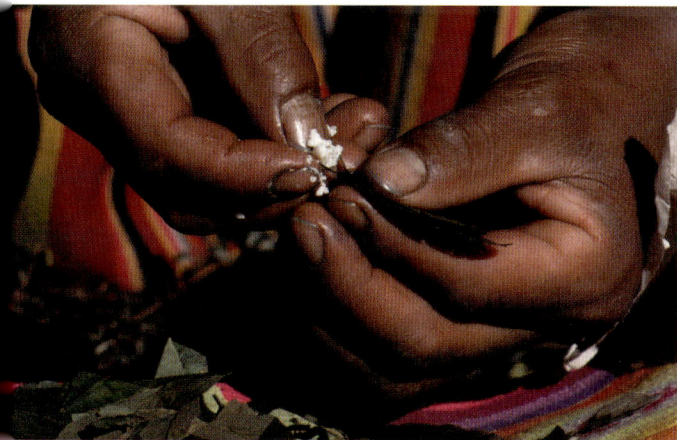

I'm an anthropologist and once when I was working in a remote area of Brazil, I ate something ¹ I _____ (eat). I was pretty sick. ² I _____ (feel) any worse, actually! I suppose ³ I _____ (have) some medicine with me, but I didn't. Anyway, the *curandeira* – the local healer – brought me the strongest of their local medicine. ⁴ I _____ (take) it straightaway, but I didn't because it smelled so bad. Of course, because of this I got much worse. So, the next day, I accepted the medicine. And after a few terrible days, I got better. Then I found out what the medicine was! I really think ⁵ I _____ (die) without it, though.

11 Pronunciation *should have* and *could have*

a ▶ 100 Listen to the sentences with *could have* and *should have* from Exercise 10. Notice the weak form of *have* /həv/.

b ▶ 100 Listen again and repeat the sentences.

Wordbuilding prefixes *in-, un-, im-*

▶ **WORDBUILDING prefixes *in-, un-, im-***

We can add *in-* and *un-* to the beginning of some adjectives to mean 'not'. We can also use *im-* before some adjectives which begin with the letter 'p'.
an inappropriate place, an unexpected experience, It was impossible.

For further practice, see Workbook page 99.

---

12 Look at the wordbuilding box. Replace the words in bold with an adjective beginning with *in-, un-* or *im-*.

1 We might see an elephant today, but it's **not likely**.
2 The guide is great even though he's **not experienced**.
3 In my country, it's **not polite** to speak while you're eating.
4 I hate sleeping in a tent – it's cold and **not comfortable.**
5 Don't worry about what to wear. The invitation says it's **not formal.**
6 My colleague is friendly, but he's **not patient.**

Speaking ⎰my life⎱

13 Look at the problems you may have when doing some activities and write down one or two solutions for each one. Then talk to other students and find what advice they would give for one of the problems.

Activity	Problem
doing homework	couldn't find information
packed a suitcase	didn't have enough room
took photos	came out blurry
making a meal	burned everything
went to visit a friend	got lost

14 Work in pairs. Compare the advice you were given and decide which was the best advice.

12c The legacy of the samurai

Reading

1 How much do you know about the samurai? Work in pairs. Try to answer the questions.

1 Who were the samurai?
2 Where were they from?
3 When did they live?
4 What did they do?

2 Before you read about the samurai, look at these words. Work in pairs and make connections between the words.

army	duty	fighting	enemies
generals	martial arts		opponents
soldiers	sword	weapon	

An army is made up of soldiers.

3 Read the article about the samurai. Check your answers from Exercise 1. Find the words in Exercise 2.

4 According to the article, are these statements true (T) or false (F)?

1 The early samurai were similar to European knights.
2 The samurai eventually died out following their defeat in battle.
3 Samurai soldiers had a wide range of cultural interests.
4 The military skills of the samurai have been lost.
5 The legacy of the samurai has spread outside Japan.

5 Find these words in the article. Look at how they are used and try to guess their meaning. Then replace the words in bold in the sentences (1–6) with these words.

battle-weary (line 29)	appeal (line 51)
unarmed (line 39)	lone (line 53)
overcoming (line 44)	fierce (line 61)

1 I don't understand the **attraction** of war films.
2 I think I'm **winning against** my opponent.
3 That boxer is frightening. He's so **intense and aggressive**.
4 The army was **exhausted after the attack**.
5 We fought **without any weapons**.
6 The police say they're looking for a **single, unaccompanied** gunman.

Critical thinking relevance

6 Which of these sentences could be included as additional information? Where should the sentences go in the article?

1 His words might easily have been spoken by a Bushido master from three centuries ago.
2 The samurai promised to be loyal to these men, who needed soldiers to protect and increase their power.
3 In the late thirteenth century, a large Mongol army under the command of Kublai Khan, grandson of the Asian conqueror Genghis Khan, attacked Japan from the sea.
4 Samurai also played *Go*, a board game about land conquest.
5 The classic film *Seven Samurai* by Japanese director Akira Kurosawa has been described as one of the most influential films ever made.

Word focus *go*

7 Look at these extracts from the article. What do the expressions with *go* mean? Choose the correct option (a–c).

1 The original samurai were soldiers **who went into battle** riding horses.
  a fought   b sat   c travelled
2 Things **didn't go well** for the samurai.
  a didn't move b were fine   c weren't good
3 Samurai fighting skills **went into decline**.
  a improved   b influenced others c weakened
4 The 'samurai' is asked if he would like to **go back in time.**
  a return home b return to the past c start again

8 Work in pairs. What do the expressions with *go* mean in these sentences?

1 The battle plan **went wrong** and ended in disaster.
2 The battle **went on** for six days non-stop.
3 The number of injured soldiers **is going up** daily.
4 Suddenly, everything **went quiet**.
5 We've decided to **go ahead** with our plan.
6 I'm going to **have a go at** flower arranging.

Speaking ⟨ my life ⟩

9 Would you like to go back in time and experience life in a different age and country? Or would you prefer to live in the future? Think about these points.

- when and where
- why that time appeals to you
- your role or position in that society
- opportunities
- possible dangers

10 Work in groups. Ask questions to find out about your classmates' time-travelling choices. What is more popular – the past or the future?

▶ 101

The Legacy of the
SAMURAI

Samurai history

The samurai (the word means 'one who serves') were the elite soldier class of Japan for nearly seven hundred years. In the tenth century, the rulers in Kyoto tried and failed to organize a conscript army. If the rulers had succeeded in this, the rich landowners might not have decided to employ private soldiers and the samurai might never have existed. The original samurai were soldiers who went into battle riding horses and fought their opponents following ancient traditions. Their customs would have seemed familiar to the European knights if they had ever met each other. Later, as the armies became larger and the fighting more violent, most samurai trained for hand-to-hand fighting. However, during a long period of peace in Japan things didn't go well for the samurai and eventually, in the 1860s, they lost their position of power in Japanese society.

Samurai identity

The sword of a samurai is a symbol of authority and luxury. It was both a weapon and an art object. This double identity mirrored the samurai themselves. As well as being soldiers, they used to socialize with artists, writers and philosophers. Samurai generals did flower arranging and went to the theatre. But of all their cultural activities, the tea ceremony was the most important. It was a slow and calm tradition. It took place in a small room where swords were forbidden, even to samurai, and it must have been very inviting to battle-weary soldiers.

Bushido

Bushido is the soldier's code. It was first written down as a kind of self-help manual during the long period of peace when samurai fighting skills went into decline. The martial arts tradition continues in Japan to this day. Millions of Japanese children still practise the classic skills of sword fighting (kendo), archery (kyudo) and hand-to-hand, unarmed fighting (jujitsu) at school. But Bushido is also a code of ethics: honour, loyalty and sacrifice. As Terukuni Uki, a martial arts teacher, explains, 'Here we teach the spirit of winning, but it's not so much defeating an opponent as overcoming one's own self. These days it seems everyone is looking for someone to blame rather than focusing on himself. Our message here is that if you try hard, at kendo or anything else, you will enjoy life.'

Samurai today

The continuing appeal of the samurai is due to a simple fact: he is one of the world's greatest action figures. He's the lone swordsman who kills dozens of enemies in the name of duty and individual glory. The samurai is the cowboy, the knight, the gladiator, and the Star Wars Jedi all rolled into one. The samurai have inspired hundreds of films, video games, comic books and TV dramas. In Japan, each spring, men put on samurai armour and act out famous samurai battles. These 'weekend' samurai look fierce and realistic, but, with their plastic goggles and swords, they wouldn't have been a threat to the real thing. One of the 'samurai' is asked if he would like to go back in time. 'Hmm,' he replies. 'They seem like better times, but I don't think they were, really. It was live or die.'

archery (n) /ˈɑːtʃəri/ the sport or fighting skill using bows and arrows
conscript (n) /ˈkɒnskrɪpt/ a soldier who is called up to fight by the authorities
ruler (n) /ˈruːlə/ the leader of a country
elite (adj) /eɪˈliːt/ the richest and most powerful people in a society
knight (n) /naɪt/ a soldier of a high status background

12d I'm so sorry!

Real life making and accepting apologies

1 Work in pairs. Do people apologize a lot in your culture? Would you apologize in these situations?

- arriving late for a meeting
- forgetting someone's name
- serving food a guest doesn't like
- not liking the food someone cooks for you
- taking someone's chair in a café
- asking someone to repeat something you didn't hear
- breaking something that belongs to someone else
- handing in some work after the deadline has passed at college
- losing something that belongs to someone else

2 You are going to listen to three conversations in which people make apologies. Look at the expressions for making and accepting apologies. What do you think the three conversations are about?

3 ▶ 102 Listen to the three conversations and check your ideas from Exercise 2.

4 ▶ 102 Listen to the conversations again. Then answer the questions.

1 What is the problem?
2 How is the situation resolved?

> ▶ **MAKING AND ACCEPTING APOLOGIES**
>
> **1**
> I'm really sorry you've gone to all this trouble.
> There's no need to apologize – it's not a problem.
> It's my fault. I'll make you something else.
>
> **2**
> I couldn't help it – I slipped.
> Don't blame me – this floor is slippery.
> Look, it was an accident! It could have happened to anyone.
> It's not your fault. Sorry I got upset.
>
> **3**
> I'm so sorry to keep you waiting.
> Don't worry about it – that service is terrible.
> Sorry about that!
> It's just one of those things – buses are unreliable!

5 Work in pairs. Do you think all of the expressions for making and accepting apologies would be appropriate in each of the three relationships? Why? / Why not?

6 Pronunciation sentence stress

a ▶ 103 Listen to the expressions for making and accepting apologies. Notice which word in black is stressed. Repeat the expressions.

b Work in pairs. Take turns to speak and respond using an appropriate expression. Pay attention to the words you stress.

1 Excuse me. This is a no smoking area.
2 I'm so sorry. I forgot to bring your book back.
3 Excuse me. That seat is taken.
4 You should have told me you didn't eat garlic!
5 Why is there no milk left?
6 I'm really sorry I didn't tell you I was coming!
7 Excuse me. Please wait until the waiter shows you to a table.
8 Sorry, we don't accept credit cards.

7 Work in pairs. Choose one of the problems in Exercise 1 or use your own idea. Decide what your relationship is and take a role each. Prepare a conversation which includes at least one apology.

8 Act out your conversation in front of another pair. Can they identify the situation and the relationship?

12e How to behave …

Writing a website article

1 Work in pairs. Have you ever spent time in an English-speaking country? Tell your partner three things (apart from the language!) you found strange or different there.

2 You are going to read an article from a website which arranges host families for foreign language students in the United Kingdom. What advice do you expect to find there? Tell your partner.

3 Read the article and see if your ideas are mentioned.

4 What do you think of the advice? Does any of it surprise you?

http://www.homestayfamily.com

How to behave with a *homestay family*

I've stayed with several families in Britain and Ireland and each of them has been different. But there are some key things I can pass on about getting the best out of your stay. I hope these things are useful!

Even though you are a paying guest in their home, take a small gift for your hosts. You'd expect a gift from a guest, I'm sure.

Your stay is not just about learning English. British and Irish people will expect you to show an interest in British and Irish culture.

Take some photos from home so that you can talk to your hosts about the photos. Taking the photos will also give you more opportunities to actually speak English.

You're not a tourist, so don't behave like a tourist. Your host family will be getting on with normal life. Normal life is what you are there to experience!

And finally, remember the importance of being punctual (two o'clock means two o'clock!), polite (be careful with expressions you've picked up from pop music and movies!) and sociable (join in with things – at least the first time).

5 Writing skill checking your writing

a Look at this list of seven things which you should use to check your writing. Has the writer of the website article already checked all the things?

grammar	spelling
linking words	style
organization	vocabulary
relevance	

b The writer can improve the article by avoiding some words that are repeated. Look at the first line of the article. Who or what does *them* refer to?

c Replace the other highlighted words in the article with these words. There is one extra word.

It	one	She	That	the same
their	them	there	they	This

6 Work in groups. You are going to write an article for students coming to your country. Brainstorm ideas. Use these categories or ideas that are more relevant to your culture.

- celebrations
- dress
- food
- formality
- greetings
- house rules
- meal times
- money

7 Work on your own. Choose three to five ideas from your list in Exercise 6. Write an article of 150–200 words.

8 Use the list in Exercise 5a to check and revise your article.

9 Exchange articles with the other members of your group. Which were the most common topics?

my life ▶ DECISIONS ▶ WHERE DID I GO WRONG? ▶ GOING BACK IN TIME ▶ MAKING AND ACCEPTING APOLOGIES
▶ A WEBSITE ARTICLE

77

12f Shark vs. octopus

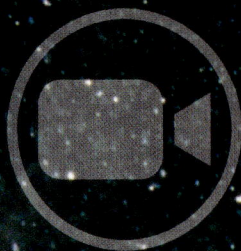

A giant Pacific octopus interacts with a scuba diver in the North Pacific Ocean.

Before you watch

1 Work in groups. Look at the photo and the caption. Discuss the questions.

1. What do you know about this animal?
2. How would you feel if you were the diver? Why?
3. Which animal would frighten you more: an octopus or a shark? Why?
4. What do you think might happen in a meeting between an octopus and a shark?

2 Key vocabulary

a Read the sentences. The words in bold are used in the video. Guess the meaning of the words.

1. We have a **tank** with eight different kinds of tropical fish in it. They're beautiful to look at.
2. Mice can be killed by several **predators**, such as foxes and birds, and of course, cats.
3. A tiger's stripes help to **camouflage** it as it moves through grass and bushes.
4. Polar bears are the same colour as their **surroundings** in winter, when everything is white.
5. Some animals **release** a strong smell when they are in danger.

b Match the words in bold in Exercise 2a with these definitions.
   a. to use patterns and colours so that it's difficult to be seen
   b. the place where you are and the things that are there
   c. to allow a liquid or gas to escape
   d. animals that kill and eat other animals to survive
   e. a large container of water to keep fish and similar animals in

While you watch

3 [▷ 12.1] Watch the video and check your ideas from Exercise 1 question 4. Are you surprised?

4 [▷ 12.1] Work in pairs, Student A and Student B. Watch the first part of the video (0.00–1.38) again. Make notes about your animal. Then tell your partner.

Student A: the spiny dogfish shark

1. usual food

2. how it gets its name

3. usual behaviour

Student B: the giant Pacific octopus

4. three ways it keeps itself safe from predators

5. usual food

5 [▷ 12.1] Try to complete the summary of what happened in the tank. Watch the video again to check your answers if necessary.

The spiny dogfish shark is a predator, but the octopus is not its usual prey. If it was, the aquarium staff wouldn't have put them in the same ¹ _____ . But then, dead ² _____ started to appear at the bottom of the tank. The ³ _____ were worried. But then they discovered that the ⁴ _____ was attacking the ⁵ _____ . Nobody had expected this to happen. The octopus was more dangerous than the sharks!

After you watch

6 Vocabulary in context

a [▷ 12.2] Watch the clips from the video. Choose the correct meaning of the words and phrases.

b Answer the questions in your own words. Then work in pairs and compare your answers.

1. What other words can you use to get someone's attention when you start to speak?
2. Think of some well-known inventions or products. Do you know how they got their names?
3. What kind of thing do people dine on in your country?

7 Work in small groups. Brainstorm as many animals as you can in two minutes. Then discuss the connections between them – which are predators and which are prey? How many animals can you connect into a 'food chain'?

---

aquarium (n) /əˈkweəriəm/ a type of zoo for fish and other sea animals
beak (n) /biːk/ the hard part of a mouth, usually on a bird
dismiss (v) /dɪsˈmɪs/ to reject or not consider something
prey (n) /preɪ/ an animal that is killed and eaten by a predator
sucker (n) /ˈsʌkə/ part of an animal's body that helps them hold things
welfare (n) /ˈwelfeə/ health or safety of people or animals

Grammar

1 Complete the article about the photo with the correct form of the verbs.

This photo is one of the most famous photos of the rare snow leopard. What makes this photo so extraordinary? Firstly, patience. The photographer, Steve Winter, spent ten months on this assignment. If he ^{1} _____ (be) in a hurry, he ^{2} _____ (not get) his shots. Secondly, dedication. Steve camped out for six weeks at 30 degrees below zero, conditions in which he ^{3} _____ (freeze) to death! Next, cooperation. Steve credited the knowledge of local experts Tashi Tundup and Raghu Chundawat, without whom he ^{4} _____ (not be able) to go ahead with the project. Finally, the animal itself. Steve says the photo 'was a real collaboration between the snow leopard and myself'. And it's true. Imagine how differently the photo ^{5} _____ (turn out) if the snow leopard ^{6} _____ (not go) hunting, slowly and silently, on that snowy night.

2 Read the article again. Which statements are true, according to the information given?

1 A combination of factors led to the success of the photo.
2 Steve Winter nearly died on this assignment.
3 Winter needed help to find the leopard.
4 The photo shows the leopard while it's hunting.

3 **>> MB** Work in pairs. Read the sentences about Steve Winter. Discuss what would/might/could have happened if the situations had been different.

1 His first camera was a gift from his father on his seventh birthday.
2 The snow leopard has a reputation for being impossible to find.
3 Steve didn't get any shots until he moved higher up the mountain.

I CAN	
talk about things that did not happen (*should have* and *could have*)	☐
talk about the hypothetical results of things that did not happen (third conditional)	☐

Vocabulary

4 Write adjectives with the correct prefix which mean the same as:

1 not appropriate _____
2 not comfortable _____
3 not experienced _____
4 not formal _____
5 not likely _____
6 not patient _____
7 not polite _____
8 not possible _____
9 not expected _____

5 Write sentences with four of the adjectives from Exercise 4.

6 **>> MB** Work in pairs. Tell your partner about a time when:

- something went wrong
- you had a go at something new
- something went on for longer than you expected
- something went up in price or number very quickly

I CAN	
use negative prefixes correctly	☐
talk about things with expressions with *go*	☐

Real life

7 Work in pairs. Complete the exchanges with these expressions. Then continue the conversations.

Don't worry about it –	It's not your fault.
No, it's my fault.	Well, don't blame me –

1 A: I'm so sorry I forgot to call you last night.
  B: _____ I wasn't at home anyway.

2 A: Oh, no. We haven't got any orange juice left.
  B: _____ I don't even drink it.

3 A: I'm really sorry about getting upset yesterday.
  B: _____ I shouldn't have shouted!

4 A: Sorry about the problem the other day.
  B: _____ You did nothing wrong.

I CAN	
make and accept apologies	☐

UNIT 9a Exercise 10, page 35

Student A

1 Complete the sentences with the passive form of the verb in brackets.

2 Read the sentences to your partner. Student B must decide if the sentences are true or false.

3 Listen to your partner's sentences. Decide if they are true or false. (Your sentence 3 is false.)

1 Same-day shipping _____ by over 80 per cent of online shoppers nowadays. (*demand*, present simple)
2 By 2030, a mobile device _____ by three out of four people globally. (*own*, future)
3 By 2030, cash _____ no longer _____ in most stores in Europe. (*accept*, future)
4 More and more brands _____ to show that their products are ethical and this will continue into the future. (*expect*, present continuous)
5 In the next few years, over a quarter of all purchases _____ following recommendations on social media. (*make*, future)

UNIT 10a Exercise 9, page 47

Pair A

1 Think of one example for each of these categories. Write at least four clues for two of your examples using the second conditional.

- a job
- a famous person
- an animal
- a country

job – airline pilot
If we did this job, we'd spend a lot of time travelling.

2 Read the sentences to Pair B. They must guess your job, person, etc. Be prepared to give extra clues.

3 Listen to Pair B's sentences. Guess the job, person, etc.

UNIT 11a Exercise 10, page 59

Pair A

Read the news story. Write a short conversation between the man and a rescuer. Practise your conversation so that you are ready to act it out for Pair B. Then turn back to page 59.

A walker who got lost in the hills was rescued this weekend after taking a photo with his phone and emailing it to the Volunteer Rescue Service. The man had fallen and was injured, but with no maps he couldn't tell the rescuers where he was. He took the photo after advice from the rescue team, who then recognized the location immediately.

UNIT 11c Exercise 12, page 62

Pair A

Read the notes. Practise describing the apps in your pair and make up a name for the app. Then tell Pair B about them. Pair B must decide which app doesn't exist. App 3 is the one that doesn't exist.

1 audio clips of different sounds – when you need to invent a reason to end a conversation
2 food app – tells you how many calories in food
3 clean clothes app – tells you when clothes are dirty and need washing

UNIT 9a Exercise 10, page 35
Student B

1 Complete the sentences with the passive form of the verb in brackets.

2 Listen to your partner's sentences. Decide if they are true or false.

3 Read the sentences to your partner. Student A must decide if the sentences are true or false. (Your sentence 3 is false.)

1 The amount of money which _____ by the middle classes around the world will triple by 2030. (*spend*, present simple)
2 By 2030, over $500 billion _____ via mobile payments, compared to $75 billion in 2016. (*spend*, future)
3 Larger and larger stores _____ to meet increasing demand from shoppers. (*build*, future)
4 Delivery in 1–3 hours _____ by over 60 per cent of online shoppers nowadays. (*request*, present continuous)
5 Personal information _____ with retailers by the majority of shoppers in the next few years. (*share*, future)

UNIT 10a Exercise 9, page 47
Pair B

1 Think of one example for each of these categories. Write at least four clues for two of your examples using the second conditional.

- a job
- a famous person
- an animal
- a country

job – airline pilot
If we did this job, we'd spend a lot of time travelling.

2 Listen to Pair A's sentences. Guess the job, person, etc.

3 Read your sentences to Pair A. They must guess your job, person, etc. Be prepared to give extra clues.

UNIT 11a Exercise 10, page 59
Pair B

Read the news story. Write a short conversation between Adam and Corey. Practise your conversation so that you are ready to act it out for Pair A. Then turn back to page 59.

A message in a bottle which was put into the Atlantic Ocean in Florida has reached Ireland. Adam Flannery, aged 17, found the bottle which had been sent by high school student Corey Swearingen. The message gave Corey's contact details and asked the finder to get in touch with details of where the bottle ended up.

UNIT 11c Exercise 12, page 62
Pair B

Read the notes. Practise describing the apps in your pair and make up a name for the app. Then tell Pair A about them. Pair A must decide which app doesn't exist. App 2 is the one that doesn't exist.

1 how much sun cream? – tells you how sunny it is
2 late homework excuses – gives you different things to say to your teacher
3 positive messages – sent to your phone each day. 'I'm wonderful', etc.

GRAMMAR SUMMARY
UNITS 7–12

used to, would and past simple

used to

We use *used to* to talk about past habits and states.
> We **used to** go on holiday to California every year when I was a kid. (= past habit)
> They **used to** have a really tiny flat in the city centre. (= past state)

Used to is always followed by the infinitive. We use the same form for all persons (*I*, *you*, *he/she/it*, etc.). In negatives and questions, we use *use to* not *used to*.
> There **didn't use to** be so much traffic here.
> **Did** you **use to** live near the sea?

We often use adverbs of frequency and other time phrases with *used to*.
> We used to eat there **every week**.

We often use *used to* to describe past actions and states that aren't true any more.
> I used to live in Germany. (= I don't live there now.)
> She used to watch a lot of TV. (= She doesn't watch much TV any more.)

We sometimes use frequency adverbs with *used to*. They come before *used to*.
> We **always** used to go to the seaside in the summer when I was a child.

To talk about habits in the present, we use the present simple with *usually*.
> We **usually** go for a walk in the park every day. (not ~~We use to go for a walk ...~~)

We don't normally use *used to* for repeated actions that lasted a short period of time. We use the past simple instead.
> I **cycled** to work every day last week. (not ~~I used to cycle to work every day last week.~~)

▶ **Exercise 1**

would

We also use *would* + infinitive to talk about repeated past actions. In spoken English, *would* often becomes *'d*.
> I**'d** spend every day in summer outside when I was a child.

We only use *would* to talk about repeated actions in the past. We don't use *would* to talk about states.
> We **used to** own a really nice house in the countryside. (not ~~We'd own a house ...~~)

We sometimes use frequency adverbs with *would*. They come after *would*.
> I'd **always** do my homework at the last minute when I was at school.

When we talk about the past, we often start with *used to* and then continue with *would*.
> When I first moved to London, I **used to** go out a lot. I**'d** visit museums and go to concerts. I**'d** eat out at least once a week …

▶ **Exercises 2 and 3**

Comparison: adverbs

more/less + adverb

To make comparative forms of adverbs, we use *more* + adverb (+ *than*).
> This room gets warm **more quickly** than the rest of the house.
> You can live **more cheaply** in other parts of the city.

The opposite of *more* + adverb is *less* + adverb.
> You clean the flat **less often** than me.

Some comparative adverb forms are irregular. They have the same form as the comparative adjective. For example, *well → better, badly → worse, far → further, fast → faster, high → higher, early → earlier, late → later, soon → sooner*.

▶ **Exercise 4**

(not) as + adverb + as

To make comparisons, we also use *(not) as* + adverb + *as*. *Not* normally goes with the verb.
> Martina can run **as fast as** Silvia. (= Martina and Silvia can run at the same speed.)
> I don**'t** go out **as often as** I did in the past. (= I used to go out more often.)

▶ **Exercise 5**

Comparison: patterns

To say that a situation is changing, we use comparative + *and* + comparative. We can use a comparative adjective or a comparative adverb in this structure.
> It's getting **colder and colder** – it's probably going to snow. (comparative adjective – one syllable)
> Things are becoming **more and more expensive** in this country. (comparative adjective – longer adjective)
> I've got so much work that I'm going to bed **later and later**. (comparative adverb)

Remember that we add *-er* to most one-syllable adjectives, and we put *more* before longer adjectives to make the comparative adjective form.

We often use *more and more* + noun.
> **More and more people** cycle to work these days.

To say that two things change at the same time, we use comparative + clause, *the* + comparative + clause.
> The harder you work, the more success you have. (= If you work hard, you'll be more successful.)
> The worse the weather is, the more traffic there is. (= When the weather is bad, the traffic gets bad too.)

We sometimes use this structure with only a noun phrase instead of a clause, or with only a comparative form.
> The taller the mountain, the greater the difficulty. (= Tall mountains are more difficult to climb.)
> The more the merrier. (= When there are lots of people, everyone is happier.)

▶ **Exercise 6**

Exercises

1 Complete the sentences with the correct form of *used to* and these verbs.

> do   drive   listen   live   love   own
> not be   not feel

1 I _____ in Lima when I was young.
2 What _____ you _____ at the weekends when you were a child?
3 We _____ going to the theatre when we lived in London.
4 There _____ any houses here when I was young – it was all fields.
5 I _____ worried when I had an exam at school.
6 We _____ a lovely house by the sea.
7 _____ people _____ more before they built a metro here?
8 She _____ to rock music before she went to university.

2 Tick the sentences in which *used to* can be replaced by *would*.

1 I didn't use to like classical music when I was a teenager, but now I love it.
2 We used to visit Los Angeles often before we had children.
3 Their music used to sound very different before the new guitarist joined the band.
4 When I was younger, I used to believe in UFOs, but I don't any more.
5 Sean used to play basketball every day when he was a teenager.
6 My family used to go to the same holiday resort every year when I was a child.

3 Complete the conversation with the *used to, would* or past simple form of the verbs in brackets.

A: You've been to Hamburg, haven't you?
B: Yes, I [1] _____ (go) there often for work when I was living in Germany. Are you going to visit?
A: Yeah, next month. Any recommendations?
B: Well, I [2] _____ (leave) Germany in 2012. Things might be different now. But, I remember we [3] _____ (eat) in a great Italian restaurant. It was by the river. I can't remember the name, but they [4] _____ (make) fantastic pizza.
A: OK, I'll look for it. Anything else?
B: Well, I remember I once [5] _____ (visit) the modern art gallery with my company. It was excellent. I think they always [6] _____ (take) visitors there.
A: OK, thanks. Any other advice?
B: Yes – walk everywhere! The city centre is quite small. I never [7] _____ (use) public transport when I was there.

4 Complete the sentences with the correct comparative form of the adverbs in brackets. Sometimes, you will need to use irregular comparative forms.

1 Jack always wins when they race. Jack runs _____ than John. (quickly)
2 Ruth is the laziest person in her family. Ruth works _____ than her brothers. (hard)
3 Your motorbike is really noisy. Your motorbike runs _____ than mine. (quietly)
4 The last flight is the Fastair flight. The Fastair flight arrives _____ than all the others. (late)
5 Katy is a very slow worker. Sarah doesn't work _____ than Katy. (slowly)
6 Mike exercises once a week, but Martin exercises every day. Mike exercises _____ than Martin. (often)
7 Julie's exam result was better than the other students' results. Julie did _____ in the exam than the others. (well)

5 Complete the sentences so that they mean the same as the sentences in Exercise 4. Use (*not*) *as … as* and the verbs and adverbs in brackets.

1 John _____ Jack. (run quickly)
2 Ruth _____ her brothers. (work hard)
3 Your motorbike _____ mine. (run quietly)
4 The other flights _____ the Fastair flight. (arrive late)
5 Katy _____ Sarah. (work quickly)
6 Mike _____ Martin. (exercise often)
7 The other students _____ Julie in the exam. (do well)

6 Match the statements (1–6) with the replies (a–f).

1 I could only find this birthday cake. Is it too big?
2 I want to get fit, but jogging is so hard!
3 There's so much traffic on the roads these days.
4 What time shall we go for lunch?
5 The price of flats is so high here at the moment.
6 Why are you doing another course?

a I know – more and more people are driving.
b It's fine – the bigger, the better!
c The earlier the better – I'm already feeling hungry!
d Yes, it's getting harder and harder to buy somewhere to live.
e The more qualifications you have, the easier it is to get a job.
f The more you run, the easier it'll get.

GRAMMAR SUMMARY UNIT 8

Verb patterns: *-ing* form and *to* + infinitive

When we put two verbs together in a sentence, the form of the second verb depends on the first. After many verbs we use the *-ing* form.

> I **love** travelling abroad.
> I **can't stand** waiting in queues.

Other common verbs followed by the *-ing* form: *adore, avoid, can't help, can't stand, describe, don't mind, enjoy, fancy, finish, imagine, keep, mention, miss, practise, recommend, spend (time/money), suggest.*
The negative of the *-ing* form is *not + -ing*.

> I **enjoy not getting** up early at the weekend.

After many other verbs, we use a verb in the *to* + infinitive form.

> I **hope to see** you later this year.
> It **seems to be** a good destination.

Other common verbs followed by the *to* + infinitive form: *agree, arrange, ask, can't afford, choose, decide, expect, fail, hope, intend, learn, manage, need, offer, plan, pretend, promise, refuse, seem, threaten, want, would like, would love, would prefer.*

The negative of *to* + infinitive is *not + to* + infinitive.

> I promise **not to be** late.

These verbs can be followed by both the *to* + infinitive and *-ing* form, with no difference in meaning: *begin, continue, hate, like, love, prefer, start.*

> I **began reading** the book. (or I **began to read** …)

▶ **Exercises 1 and 2**

Other uses

We use the *-ing* form when we use a verb as the subject of a sentence.

> **Travelling** can be very educational.

We also use the *-ing* form when a verb follows a preposition.

> I'm usually good **at finding** cheap hotels.
> We often **think about travelling** for a year.

We often use *to* + infinitive after an adjective.

> It was **amazing to visit** Chile for the first time.

▶ **Exercise 3**

Present perfect simple and continuous

Form

We form the present perfect simple with *have/has* + past participle of the main verb. (See page 96 for a list of common irregular past participles.)

> I've just **got** back from holiday.

We form the present perfect continuous with *have/has* + *been* + *-ing* form of the main verb.

For example: *I've been waiting, he's been doing, they haven't been reading.*

▶ **Exercise 4**

Use

We use both the present perfect simple and the present perfect continuous to talk about something that started in the past and continues in the present. We use:

- the present perfect simple to talk about a state that started in the past and continues in the present.
  *I've **loved** Turkey since I first visited in 2005.*

- the present perfect continuous to talk about a long action or a repeated action that started in the past and continues in the present.
  *I've **been waiting** for your email since last week.* (long action)
  *We've **been coming** here for years.* (repeated action)

We also use both the present perfect simple and the present perfect continuous to talk about actions in the past that have an effect on the present. We use:

- the present perfect simple to talk about short actions that are complete and that have an effect on the present.
  *Joel **has broken** his arm.* (= it's still broken)

- the present perfect continuous to talk about long actions in the past that have an effect on the present.
  *We've **been walking** in the forest all morning.* (= and now we're hungry and tired)

We often use the present perfect continuous to emphasize the duration of a longer past activity and the present perfect simple to talk about its final result.

> *I've **been researching** holidays all morning. I think I've **found** the perfect one for us.* (*researching* = longer activity, *found* = result)

For other uses of the present perfect simple, see Split Edition A, Unit 2.

Remember that we don't normally use stative verbs in the continuous. See Split Edition A, Unit 1.

▶ **Exercise 5**

How long … ?

We make questions with *how long* to ask about duration. We use:

- *how long* + present perfect simple to ask about a state which started in the past and continues in the present.
  How long have you known David?

- *how long* + present perfect continuous to ask about an action or a repeated action which started in the past and continues in the present.
  How long have you been doing conservation work?

- *how long* + past simple to ask about a state or action that is now finished.
  How long did you live in Africa?

We use *for* in answers to questions in all three tenses, but we can't use *since* with the past simple.

> *I lived in Africa for ten years.* (not *… since 2002.*)

▶ **Exercise 6**

Exercises

1 Choose the correct option to complete the sentences. Sometimes, both options are possible.

1 Do you fancy *going / to go* to the cinema tonight?
2 He's pretending *being / to be* sick so that he doesn't have to go to work.
3 She'd prefer *not speaking / not to speak* to anyone at the moment.
4 I love *to swim / swimming* in the sea at night.
5 Can you imagine *having / to have* as much money as a famous actor?
6 I hate *to have / having* to rush in the morning.
7 I recommend *visiting / to visit* the history museum. It's fascinating.
8 They've chosen *not having / not to have* a party for their wedding anniversary.

2 Complete the conversation with the correct form of the verbs in brackets.

A: I'm going on holiday soon!
B: Oh, you're so lucky. I'd really love
   ¹ .... (go) away somewhere! Where are you going?
A: To Spain. I'm going to spend all day
   ² .... (lie) on a beach! What are you going to do in the summer holidays?
B: Well, I can't afford ³ .... (travel) very far, but I'm hoping ⁴ .... (go) camping somewhere near here.
A: At least you won't have to get on a plane. I can't stand ⁵ .... (fly)!
B: Really? Well, when you're on the plane, just avoid ⁶ .... (think) about where you are. Just relax and imagine ⁷ .... (sit) on a beach.
A: I'll try. Well, anyway, I'm going to enjoy
   ⁸ .... (not work) for a few weeks!

3 Complete the text with the correct form of these verbs.

drive	eat	get	take	use	visit	walk

If you're keen on ¹ .... a break from modern life, then La Posada del Inca Eco-Lodge may be the place for you. It's on one of the most beautiful islands on Lake Titicaca, in Bolivia.
² .... here is impossible because it is a car-free island. This means it's great ³ .... if you enjoy ⁴ .... , especially as the views are spectacular. It is possible ⁵ .... all your meals in the hotel; the food is simple but delicious. The rooms don't have fridges, TVs or wi-fi, but they do have hot water and heating. It is difficult ⁶ .... an internet connection on the island, but if you really need ⁷ .... the internet, then you'll have to climb up to the restaurants near the top of the hill.

4 Write sentences and questions with the present perfect continuous form.

1 I / live / here / since / 2015.
  ....
2 She / not wait / long.
  ....
3 you / work / all day?
  ....
4 They / swim / for / about an hour.
  ....
5 I / not listen / to the radio.
  ....
6 he / play computer games / all morning?
  ....

5 Choose the correct option to complete the sentences.

1 I've already *eaten / been eating*, so I don't need any dinner.
2 We've *come / been coming* to this island since I was a child.
3 He's *had / been having* that car for ages.
4 I haven't *seen / been seeing* Jack for three years.
5 She's *studied / been studying* all afternoon and now she needs a break.
6 Sorry, have you *waited / been waiting* for ages?
7 We haven't *known / been knowing* each other for long.
8 I travel a lot. I've *visited / been visiting* ten countries.

6 Complete the conversation with the present perfect simple or present perfect continuous of the verbs in brackets.

A: You look tired. What ¹ .... (you / do)?
B: I ² .... (search) on the internet for hours for a holiday destination. And I still ³ .... (not find) anywhere!
A: What about the usual place you go?
B: Oh, I ⁴ .... (go) to that resort for the last five years. I'm bored with it!
A: Well, why don't you go on a cycling holiday?
B: A cycling holiday?! I'm not sure …
   ⁵ .... (you / go) on one before?
A: Yes. I went on an organized tour around Rajasthan last year. It was the most amazing holiday I ⁶ .... ever .... (have)!
B: Really? It sounds very tiring!
A: It was fun! And I made new friends. We ⁷ .... (stay) in touch since our holiday. I ⁸ .... (already book) my next cycling holiday with the same company.
B: How long ⁹ .... (you / do) these tours?
A: Oh, for a long time. They're very good. You should come with me! You'd love it!
B: Well, yes, but I ¹⁰ .... (not have) much time to exercise recently.
A: That's OK. I'm going in six months. You can start cycling tomorrow!

Passives

Verbs can be active or passive. We normally use the active form when the focus of the sentence is on the 'agent' – the person or thing that does an action.

> **All kinds of people** buy products like these. (focus = all kinds of people)

When we use the passive, a sentence isn't about the agent any more. The passive emphasizes the action.

> **Products like these** are bought by all kinds of people. (focus = products like these)

Form

When we use the passive, the object of the active sentence becomes the subject of the passive sentence.

> All kinds of people buy <u>products like these</u>.
> OBJECT
> <u>Products like these</u> **are bought** by all kinds of people.
> SUBJECT

We form the passive with a form of the auxiliary verb *be* and the past participle of the main verb.

Tense	Active	Passive
Present simple	*buy*	*is/are bought*
Present continuous	*is/are buying*	*is/are being bought*
Past simple	*bought*	*is/was bought*
Past continuous	*was/were buying*	*was/were being bought*
Present perfect	*has/have bought*	*has/have been bought*
Past perfect	*had bought*	*had been bought*
Modal verbs	*can buy* *will buy* *etc.*	*can be bought* *will be bought* *etc.*

We can use *by* + noun to say who does or did the action in a sentence with a passive verb. This makes the information sound new or important.

> The new farmers' market was opened **by a local businessman** last month.

▶ **Exercise 1**

Use

We often use the passive:

- when it's obvious who does an action
  The letter **was delivered** *this morning.* (= obviously by the postman)

- when it's unimportant who does an action
  When I complained to the company about the camera I bought, I **was sent** *a new one.* (= it doesn't matter who sent it)

- when we don't know who does an action
  My bag **was stolen**. (= I don't know who stole it)

- when we don't want to say who does an action
  The house **hasn't been cleaned** *again.* (= I don't want to say who hasn't cleaned the house.)

▶ **Exercises 2 and 3**

Articles

We use *a/an* the first time we mention something.
> *I've just bought* **a** *new washing machine.*

We use *the* when we mention something which is known (because it has already been mentioned, for example and when there is only one of something.)
> *I bought a shirt and a tie.* **The** *shirt was quite cheap. It was warm and* **the** *sun was shining.*

We use no article (**zero article**) to talk in general about uncountable or plural nouns.
> **Tourism** *brings a lot of money to the country.*

▶ **Exercise 4**

Quantifiers

We use *a lot of, lots of, loads of* and *plenty of* with uncountable and plural nouns to talk about large quantities. We often use *plenty of* to mean 'more than enough'.
> *There are* **a lot of** *food shops in my neighbourhood. We don't need to go to the supermarket. There's* **plenty of** *food in the fridge.* (= more than enough food)

We also use *many* + plural noun in more formal, written English to talk about a large quantity.
> *There are* **many** *ways to save money on your shopping.*

We don't normally use *much* in affirmative sentences. However, we use *too much* with uncountable nouns and *too many* with plural nouns in both spoken English and formal writing to say there is more than we want.
> *There's* **too much** *noise here – I can't work.*

We also use *much* and *many* to ask questions about quantities.
> *Were there* **many** *nice clothes in the sale?*

We use *some* to talk about neutral, non-specific quantities with uncountable and plural nouns.
> *I've got* **some** *food.* (= not a lot, not a little)

We use *several, one or two, a couple of* and *a few* to talk about smaller quantities with plural nouns. We normally use *several* to refer to larger quantities than *one or two, a couple of* and *a few*.
> *We've got* **one or two** *questions about the offer.*
> *I've been to* **several** *nice cafés by the river.* (= five or six)

We use *a little* and *a bit of* to talk about smaller quantities with uncountable nouns.
> *We've got* **a little** *money left. Let's get some ice cream.*

We use *not any* with plural and uncountable nouns to talk about zero quantity. We also use *any* when we ask questions about uncountable and plural countable nouns.

We use *little* + uncountable noun and *few* + countable noun to say 'not much' and 'not many' in formal, written English. They have a more negative meaning than *a little* and *a few*.

▶ **Exercises 5 & 6**

Exercises

1 Are the sentences correct? If not, correct any mistakes with the passive.

1 My new book can found online or in bookshops.
2 Is the building being painted this week?
3 The hole in the roof still hasn't be repaired!
4 Your order was been sent to you ten days ago.
5 The show is watched from millions of people all over the world.
6 Our friends' food being brought to the table when we arrived.
7 Will the meeting be finished before lunch?
8 I hadn't was told about the party.

2 Choose the correct options to complete the text.

> **Great meal at Rexo!**
> This new Mexican restaurant [1] *has advertised / has been advertised* quite a lot on the radio recently, so I decided to try it. I love Mexican food anyway!
> We arrived at around 8 pm. It was really busy, but we [2] *gave / were given* a table after just five minutes. While our table [3] *was prepared / was being prepared*, we [4] *looked / were looked* at the menu. There's a great selection and the prices are good.
> After [5] *we'd ordered / we'd been ordered*, our food [6] *was brought / brought* quickly. Everything was delicious. We only had one complaint. We'd asked for a bottle of tap water. But when we paid, we saw that $2 [7] *had added / had been added* for the bottle. This didn't seem fair – tap water is free in all the other restaurants in town! But overall, I'm sure Rexo will be a success and their delicious food will [8] *enjoy / be enjoyed* by everyone!

3 Rewrite the information in the passive. Don't include the agents in brackets.

1 The supermarket has just delivered the shopping.
The shopping _____ .
2 (The technician) is fixing my computer.
My computer _____ .
3 Will (you) invite Sonia to the party?
_____ Sonia _____ to the party?
4 (We) didn't finish the work.
The work _____ .
5 (You) can't use mobile phones here.
Mobile phones _____ here.
6 The manager had called the police.
The police _____ .
7 Do (you) accept credit cards?
_____ credit cards _____ ?
8 (People) don't use the new shopping centre.
The new shopping centre _____ .

4 Complete the text with *the, a(n)* or – (zero article).

[1] _____ cash machine in [2] _____ New York had to be switched off because it was giving out too much money. [3] _____ machine, in one of [4] _____ busiest underground train stations, was giving [5] _____ ten-dollar notes instead of [6] _____ five-dollar notes. As soon as [7] _____ people realized what was happening, [8] _____ queue developed. Within thirty minutes, news of what was happening appeared on [9] _____ internet, and even more people arrived. But not long after, [10] _____ employee from the bank came to switch it off.

5 Complete the second sentences with these quantifiers so that they mean the same as the first sentences.

a couple of	a little	how much	loads of
plenty of	several	too much	

1 There's more traffic than we want in this town.
There's _____ traffic in this town.
2 There are one or two good shops in this street.
There are _____ good shops in this street.
3 I have some money left, but not very much.
I have _____ money left.
4 There are a lot of good offers in that shop.
There are _____ good offers in that shop.
5 We won't be late – we've got more time than we need.
We won't be late – we've got _____ time.
6 Four or five new restaurants have opened near my flat.
_____ restaurants have opened near my flat.
7 How many bottles of juice do we have?
_____ juice do we have?

6 Choose the correct options to complete the conversation.

A: Right, we've spent [1] *a lot of / much* money now. Let's go home.
B: Not yet. I still need to get [2] *a couple of / loads of* things – just a new dress and some shoes.
A: Really? You've already got [3] *many / plenty of* pairs of shoes at home – more than you need, in my opinion.
B: Yes, but I [4] *don't have any / have not any* shoes that match my new coat!
A: I see. Well, [5] *how much / how many* time do you need? I'm getting hungry. I only had [6] *a bit of / a couple of* breakfast.
B: I won't be long – I promise. Why don't you go to the café over there? Then I can have [7] *a little / little* time to myself.
A: Alright. I'll see you in [8] *a few / few* minutes.

Second conditional

We use the second conditional to talk about unreal situations in the present or future. The form is:

If + past simple + *would* + infinitive

*If I **liked** science, I'**d read** more books about space exploration.*
*If we **had** to live on Mars, it **wouldn't** be easy.*

We can also use *might* in the main clause when we are less sure about the result.

*If you **saw** the film, you **might** like it.*

We often use *could* in the main clause to talk about ability and possibility.

*If we lived by the sea, we **could** go swimming every day. (= we would be able to go swimming)*

When the *if* clause comes first, we use a comma between the two clauses. When the main clause comes before the *if* clause, we don't add a comma between the two clauses.

If we wanted to, we could do more to protect the planet.
We could do more to protect the planet if we wanted to.

We don't normally put *would* in the *if* clause. We normally use a past tense.

*If I **had** more time, I would go travelling more often.*
(not *If I would have more time, ...*)

When we put *be* in the *if* clause, we can use *were* instead of *was*. We normally do this when we use the phrase 'If I were you' to give advice.

*If I **were you**, I wouldn't take the job.*

We also use *were* in this way in other sentences. This normally sounds more formal, but some people consider it more correct.

*If I **were** richer, I'd become a space tourist.*
*If he **were** more careful, he wouldn't have so many accidents.*

▶ Exercises 1, 2 and 3

Defining relative clauses

We use defining relative clauses to say exactly which person, thing, place or time we are talking about.

*That's the doctor **that I saw last month**. (relative clause tells us which doctor)*

that, which and who

To introduce a relative clause, we use a relative pronoun or relative adverb after a noun. The choice of relative pronoun depends on the type of noun:

* for things, use *that* or *which*
  *This is the finger **that/which** hurts.*

* for people, use *that* or *who*
  *The people **that/who** spoke to us are here.*

We can leave out *that*, *which* and *who* when they are the object of the verb in the relative clause.

*She loves **the flowers (that/which)** you brought.*
(that/which = object of brought)
***The person (that/who)** you know isn't here.*

We can't leave out the relative pronoun if it's the subject of the relative clause.

*That's **the film that** won five Oscars last year.*
(not That's the film won ...)

▶ Exercise 4

whose, when and where

We use the relative pronoun *whose* to talk about possession.

*Sonia has a daughter **whose** dream is to become a doctor.*

We also make relative clauses with the relative adverbs *where* and *when*. They mean the same as preposition + *which*.

*That's the hospital **where** I was born. (= the hospital **in which** I was born)*
*Do you remember the moment **when** you decided to become a nurse? (= the moment **in which** you decided to become a nurse)*

▶ Exercises 5 and 6

Exercises

1 Match the beginnings of the sentences (1–8) with the endings (a–h).

1 If I were you,
2 People wouldn't feel so stressed
3 If my sister didn't buy so many things,
4 Which sport would you do
5 If Paul didn't drink so much coffee,
6 If my parents lived closer,
7 I wouldn't have to use public transport
8 If space travel were cheaper,

a I could visit them more often.
b she'd have more money.
c if you had more free time?
d I'd find another flat.
e if they didn't work so much.
f he might sleep better at night.
g would more people try it?
h if I had a car.

2 Choose the correct form to complete the sentences.

1 If you *were / would b*e a millionaire, what *would / did* you buy first?
2 People would *feel / felt* happier here if it *were / would be* sunnier.
3 If we *lived / would live* in the countryside, *we'll / we'd* be able to see the stars at night.
4 If I *hadn't / didn't have* so much work to do, *I'd go / I went* to bed earlier.
5 I *can / could* buy a new car if *I'd save / I saved* more money.
6 My dad *would have / had* more friends if *he'd be / he was* more friendly.
7 *Would / Did* you take a job for less money if it *was / would be* closer to home?
8 If *I lived / I'd lived* nearer my work, I *could / might* walk there.

3 Complete the sentences to make second conditionals.

1 I don't exercise, so I'm not very fit.
   If I _____ more, I _____ fitter.
2 She doesn't have his number, so she can't call him.
   If she _____ his number, she _____ him.
3 You're tired because you don't get enough sleep.
   You _____ tired if you _____ enough sleep.
4 He doesn't study, so he won't pass his exams.
   If he _____ , he _____ his exams.
5 I'm ill, so I can't go to work.
   If I _____ ill, I _____ to work.
6 She often gets headaches because she uses her computer so much.
   She _____ headaches so often if she _____ her computer less.

4 Circle the correct relative pronoun or pronouns. Then cross out the relative pronoun(s) that can be omitted.

1 Is that the athlete *that / which / who* won the gold medal?
2 Those are the books *that / which / who* I borrowed from the library.
3 This is the website *that / which / who* has a lot of good recipes.
4 My boss doesn't like the report *that / which / who* I wrote for him.
5 I've just seen someone *that / which / who* I know.
6 This is the TV programme *that / which / who* got good reviews.

5 Complete the sentences with a relative clause.

1 This is a hotel. Leo is staying here.
   This is the hotel _____ .
2 The doctor has already seen those people.
   Those are the people _____ .
3 This man is Will. His wife likes running ultramarathons.
   Will is the man _____ .
4 The first woman won a gold medal at the Olympic games in 1900.
   1900 was the year _____ .
5 I told you about that man. He's my old school teacher.
   That man's the old school teacher _____ .
6 I got a lovely present from my sister. This is it.
   This is the lovely present _____ .

6 Complete the text with the phrases (a–f) and an appropriate relative pronoun or adverb.

a she grew up
b she was attacked
c story has inspired people
d was based on her life story
e lost her arm
f was living in a hotel nearby

Bethany Hamilton is an American professional surfer [1] _____ in a shark attack at the age of just sixteen and [2] _____ all around the world. On October 31, 2003, Bethany was surfing at a local beach in Hawaii when she was attacked. She lost sixty per cent of her blood on the way to hospital, but luckily she was saved by the medical team there, including one doctor [3] _____ . The attack was terrible, but Bethany was surfing again within a month, and in 2005, less then two years after the day [4] _____ , she won her first national surfing competition. Bethany became well known around the world when a film [5] _____ came out. Bethany is now married and has a child. Her wedding was by the sea on an island in Hawaii [6] _____ .

Reported speech

Statements

We can use direct speech or reported speech to say what someone else said.

> Direct speech: *He said, 'I'll see you later.'*
> Reported speech: *He said that he'd see me later.*

We can leave out *that*, especially in informal, spoken contexts.

> *She said she'd go.* (or *She said **that** she'd go.*)

When we use reported speech, we normally make some changes to the words the person actually said. We normally change the tense of the verb.

Direct speech	Reported speech
Present simple *Paul said, '**I want** to give you something.'*	Past simple *Paul said (that) he **wanted** to give me something.*
Present continuous *Maria said, '**I'm waiting** for the train.'*	Past continuous *Maria said (that) she **was waiting** for the train.*
Past simple *Paul said, 'I **sent** you a message.'*	Past perfect *Paul said (that) he **had sent** me a message.*
Present perfect simple *Maria said, 'I **have** just **arrived** home.'*	Past perfect simple *Maria said (that) she **had** just **arrived** home.*
will *Paul said, '**I'll** call you.'*	would *Paul said (that) he **would** call me.*
can *Maria said, 'I **can't** come.'*	could *Maria said (that) she **couldn't** come.*

The modals *might* and *would* don't change in reported speech.

> *'You **might** like it.' → Paul said I **might** like it.*
> *'We'**d** love to visit.' → Maria said they'**d** love to visit.*

When we report words that are still true at the time of reporting, we don't need to change the verb form.

> *'It'**s** a great film'. → Nic said it'**s** a great film.*
> *'I'**ve** lost my phone.' → Max said he'**s** lost his phone.*
> *(= He still hasn't found it.)*

We normally need to make changes to pronouns and adjectives, and words and expressions about time and place when we report.

pronouns: *I → he/she, we → they*
adjectives: *my → his/her, our → their, this → that*
time: *now → then, today → that day, tomorrow → the next day, yesterday → the previous day*
place: *here → there*

> *Seb said, 'We'll see **you here tomorrow**.'*
> *→ Seb said **they'd see me there the next day**.*

However, if the sentence is reported on the same day it was said, we don't need to change the verb form, the place or the time.

> *Seb said, 'We'll see **you here tomorrow**.'*
> *→ Seb said **they'll see me here tomorrow**.*

▶ **Exercise 1**

Questions

We normally use the verb *ask* to report questions. To report a *wh-* question we use normal word order (subject before verb). We don't add *do*, *does* or *did*.

> *'Where do you work? → She asked where I worked.*

To report a *yes/no* question, we add *if* or *whether* before the subject in the question.

> *'Did you read the article?' → She asked **if** I had read the article.* (or *She asked **whether** I had read ...*)

▶ **Exercises 2 and 3**

Reporting verbs

Patterns

To report statements, we use *say* and *tell*. With *tell*, we always use an object before the reported speech. The object is often a pronoun.

> *'I can't help.' → She told **them** (that) she couldn't help.*

With *say*, we never use an object before the reported speech.

> *'We don't want to come.' → They said that (they) didn't want to come. (not ~~They said me …~~)*

We also use many other verbs to report speech and thoughts. We use *ask, tell, remind, invite* with an object + *(not) to* + infinitive. The object is usually a person.

> *'Can you hold my bag?'*
> *→ She **asked** me **to hold** her bag.*
> *'Don't sit down.' → He **told** us **not to sit** down.*
> *'Remember to bring the present, Marcos.'*
> *→ She **reminded** Marcos to bring the present.*

We use *promise* and *offer* + *(not) to* + infinitive. We do not use an object with these verbs.

> *'I won't be late again.'*
> *→ He **promised not to be** late again.*
> *'Would you like me to drive you to the station?'*
> *→ She **offered to drive** me to the station.*

We can also use *promise* + *(that)* + clause.

> *He **promised that he wouldn't be** late again.*

▶ **Exercise 4**

Thoughts

To report thoughts, we use the verbs *realize, think* and *know*. They are followed by *that* + subject + verb. We sometimes leave out *that* after these verbs, especially in informal, spoken contexts.

> *I **realized** (that) I had forgotten my wallet.*
> *She **thought** (that) it looked like a nice restaurant.*
> *He **knew** (that) it wasn't the right house.*

We use the verb *wonder* to say 'ask yourself'. It is followed by *if/whether* or a question word.

> *'Has Julia come home yet?' → He **wondered if** Julia had come home yet.* (or *He wondered whether …*)
> *'Where can I leave my car?' → I **wondered where** I could leave my car.*

▶ **Exercises 5 and 6**

Exercises

1 Choose the correct option to complete the reported speech sentences.

1 'I love the hotel.'
   He said *he loved / he'd loved* the hotel.
2 'We arrived late.'
   They said *they were arriving / they'd arrived* late.
3 'You might not enjoy the film.'
   She said I *might not enjoy / might not have enjoyed* the film.
4 'We're leaving soon.'
   They said they *were leaving / left* soon.
5 'I can't come.'
   He said he *couldn't come / can't came*.
6 'We've just got home.'
   They said *they just got / they'd just got* home.

2 Put the words in order to make reported questions. There is one extra word that you don't need.

1 Jo asked (had / seen / if / the film / been / I)
   She asked _____ .
2 Barbara asked (did / lived / I / where)
   She asked _____ .
3 Tina asked me (Luke / if / was / had / to / I / spoken)
   She asked me _____ .
4 Enzo asked (leaving / why / were / being / we)
   He asked _____ .
5 Jaime asked (was / where / hungry / I / if)
   He asked _____ .
6 The men asked us (whether / wanted / we / did / something)
   They asked us _____ .

3 Complete the story with the reported speech form of the direct speech.

I was on the train last week when I saw my old boss. I said 'hi'. He asked [1] _____ . I told him that [2] _____ , but that we [3] _____ for years. He said that [4] _____ and asked me [5] _____ . I said [6] _____ , but that [7] _____ . He asked me [8] _____ . I said that [9] _____ , but that [10] _____ . In the end, he gave me a job!

1 'Do I know you?'
2 'We worked together.'
3 'We haven't seen each other for years.'
4 'I remember.'
5 'How are you?'
6 'I was fine.'
7 'I'm looking for a job.'
8 'Would you like an interview today?'
9 'I can't.'
10 'I'll be free tomorrow.'

4 Complete the sentences with these reporting verbs.

asked	invited	offered	reminded	said
told				

1 'I can lend you some money.'
   She _____ to lend me some money.
2 'Would you like to go to the theatre?'
   He _____ me to go to the theatre.
3 'Do you need some help?'
   She _____ if I needed some help.
4 'Don't forget to call me later.'
   I _____ him to call me later.
5 'It's a nice film.'
   He _____ that it was a nice film.
6 'I don't want to stay.'
   I _____ her that I didn't want to stay.

5 Choose the correct option to complete the sentences. Both options are possible in one sentence.

1 He asked *me to help / that I help* to fix his car.
2 They reminded *us to / that we* bring our dictionaries.
3 I wondered what *to cause / was causing* the delay.
4 He realized *to leave / that he'd left* his bag at home.
5 We invited *to go / them to go* on holiday with us.
6 She promised *to call / that she'd call* straight away.

6 The direct speech in these sentences is spoken to you. Complete the reported speech. Use the past simple form of the reporting verbs in brackets.

1 'Don't leave your bag there.' (tell)
   She _____ there.
2 'Did I forget my passport?' (wonder)
   I _____ passport.
3 'I'll never lie to you again.' (promise)
   She _____ again.
4 'Oh dear. We've left the map at home.' (realize)
   They _____ at home.
5 'Can you give me your email address?' (ask)
   He _____ email address.
6 'Would you like me to carry your bag?' (offer)
   He _____ bag.
7 'Don't forget to close all the windows.' (remind)
   She _____ all the windows.
8 'Maria will love the present.' (know)
   I _____ the present.

Third conditional

We use the third conditional to talk about unreal situations in the past. The form is:

If + past perfect + *would* + *have (not)* + past participle

We use a negative verb if the past event happened and a positive verb if the event didn't happen.

> *If you**'d worked** harder, you wouldn't have failed the exam.* (= You didn't work hard. You failed the exam.)
> *If Tina **hadn't helped** me, I wouldn't have been able to finish the project.* (= Tina helped me. I finished the project.)

When the *if* clause comes first, we use a comma between the two clauses. When the main clause comes before the *if* clause, we don't add a comma between the two clauses.

> ***If** you'd invited me, I'd have come to the party.*
> *I'd have come to the party **if** you'd invited me.*

We use the contraction *'d* in spoken English and more informal writing. It can replace either *had* or *would*.

> *If I**'d** (= had) had more time, I**'d** (= would) have visited the castle again.*

We don't normally put *would* or *have* in the *if* clause. We normally use the past perfect.

> *If those people had known the area, they wouldn't have needed a map.*
> (not *If those people would have known …*)
> *They wouldn't have needed a map if they'd known the area.* (not *… if they'd have known the area.*)

▶ **Exercises 1, 2 and 3**

should have and *could have*

We use *should (not) have* + past participle to talk about regrets about past actions. We use:

- *should have* when something was the right thing to do, but we didn't do it.
  *I **should have called** you to tell you where I was.* (= I didn't call you. I regret that.)

- *shouldn't have* when something was the wrong thing to do, but we did it.
  *I **shouldn't have brought** such a heavy bag on holiday.* (= I brought a heavy bag. I regret it.)

We also use *should/shouldn't have* to criticize people's past actions.

> *You **shouldn't have** shouted at me. It was very rude.*

▶ **Exercise 4**

We use *could (not) have* + past participle to say whether something that didn't happen was possible or impossible. We use:

- *could have* when something was possible but it didn't happen.
  *You **could have** really hurt yourself!* (= You didn't hurt yourself, but it was possible.)

- *couldn't have* when something was impossible and it didn't happen.
  *We **couldn't have** come earlier – the traffic was terrible.* (= We didn't come earlier and it wasn't possible because of the traffic.)

We also use *could have* to say something was possible in the past and we're not sure if it happened.

> *He could have got lost.* (= It's possible he got lost. But I don't know what happened.)

▶ **Exercises 5 and 6**

Exercises

1 Read the sentences (1–5). Choose the correct option (a–b) to explain each sentence.

1 If you'd called me, I would have helped you.
   a You didn't call me.
   b I helped you.
2 If I hadn't been so rude, we wouldn't have had an argument.
   a We didn't have an argument.
   b I was rude.
3 I wouldn't have gone to Scotland if you hadn't recommended it.
   a I went to Scotland
   b You didn't recommend Scotland.
4 We would have missed our flight if we'd left when you wanted to.
   a We didn't miss our flight.
   b We left when you wanted to.
5 You wouldn't have been so cold if you'd brought a warm coat.
   a You brought a warm coat.
   b You were cold.

2 Match the beginnings of the sentences (1–6) with the endings (a–f). Then complete the main clauses with *would have* or *wouldn't have*.

1 If I'd had my umbrella with me,
2 If you hadn't bought that expensive new car,
3 If I'd known how boring this job was,
4 If you'd been more careful,
5 If they hadn't booked such a cheap hotel,
6 If we hadn't forgotten to bring the map,

a we _____ been able to afford a holiday.
b you _____ broken the window.
c they _____ had a better holiday.
d I _____ got wet.
e I _____ come to work here.
f we _____ got lost.

3 Complete the sentences to make third conditionals. Use contractions where possible.

1 We didn't pay attention and we got lost.
   If we _____
   _____ lost.
2 We saw lots of plants when we visited the park.
   If we _____
   _____ plants.
3 We didn't take more water because we didn't know how hot it was.
   If we _____
   _____ more water.
4 My phone didn't work, so I couldn't call for help.
   If _____
   _____ for help.
5 I went to Kenya. I met my husband there.
   If _____
   _____ my husband.

4 Complete the sentences with *should have* or *shouldn't have* and these phrases. Use the correct form of the verb.

buy a ticket	invite so many people
check it more carefully	stay up so late last night
have a bigger breakfast	tell us earlier

1 Your report was full of mistakes.
   You _____ .
2 Our house is a mess after the party.
   We _____ .
3 John just called to say he can't come.
   He _____ .
4 I was already hungry at 11 am.
   I _____ .
5 We all feel exhausted this morning.
   We _____ .
6 I got a parking fine last week.
   I _____ .

5 Complete the sentences with *could have* or *couldn't have* and the correct form of the verb in brackets.

1 Why didn't you wear a helmet when you went skiing? You _____ (hurt) yourself.
2 It's normally very hot at this time of year. We _____ (know) it would be so bad.
3 I think he _____ (win) the race, but he hadn't trained hard enough.
4 Thanks for all your help organizing the trip. I _____ (done) it without you.
5 I've been waiting an hour for you! You _____ (call) to say you'd be late.
6 I did my best, but I didn't pass the exam. I _____ (try) any harder.

6 Complete the conversation with *could have, couldn't have, should have* or *shouldn't have* and the correct form of the verbs in brackets.

A: Did you read about the woman who survived in the wild for a week after her car broke down?
B: Yes, I saw that. She was twenty kilometres from the nearest village. And she walked into the forest to find help and then got lost. I think it was a mistake to leave the car. She ¹ _____ (stay) there. They ² _____ (find) her more quickly that way.
A: I agree. And I think she ³ _____ (leave) home without telling her friends and relatives where she was going. The article says nobody knew where she was!
B: OK, but she ⁴ _____ (know) her car would break down.
A: I always tell someone if I'm going on a long journey. She ⁵ _____ (tell) at least one person – that's obvious.
B: OK. But even then, it ⁶ _____ (take) a long time to find her. She was really in the middle of nowhere.
A: That's true.

INFINITIVE	PAST SIMPLE	PAST PARTICIPLE
beat	beat	beaten
become	became	become
bend	bent	bent
bet	bet	bet
bite	bit	bitten
blow	blew	blown
break	broke	broken
bring	brought	brought
broadcast	broadcast	broadcast
build	built	built
burn	burned/burnt	burned/burnt
burst	burst	burst
cost	cost	cost
cut	cut	cut
deal	dealt	dealt
dig	dug	dug
dream	dreamed/dreamt	dreamed/dreamt
fall	fell	fallen
feed	fed	fed
fight	fought	fought
forget	forgot	forgotten
forgive	forgave	forgiven
freeze	froze	frozen
grow	grew	grown
hang	hanged/hung	hanged/hung
hide	hid	hidden
hit	hit	hit
hold	held	held
hurt	hurt	hurt
keep	kept	kept
kneel	knelt	knelt
lay	laid	laid
lead	led	led
learn	learned/learnt	learned/learnt

INFINITIVE	PAST SIMPLE	PAST PARTICIPLE
lend	lent	lent
let	let	let
lie	lay	lain
light	lit	lit
lose	lost	lost
mean	meant	meant
misunderstand	misunderstood	misunderstood
must	had to	had to
ring	rang	rung
rise	rose	risen
sell	sold	sold
set	set	set
shake	shook	shaken
shine	shone	shone
shoot	shot	shot
shrink	shrank	shrunk
shut	shut	shut
sink	sank	sunk
slide	slid	slid
smell	smelled/smelt	smelled/smelt
spell	spelled/spelt	spelled/spelt
spend	spent	spent
spill	spilled/spilt	spilled/spilt
split	split	split
spoil	spoiled/spoilt	spoiled/spoilt
spread	spread	spread
stand	stood	stood
steal	stole	stolen
stick	stuck	stuck
swear	swore	sworn
tear	tore	torn
throw	threw	thrown
wake	woke	woken
win	won	won

Unit 7

▶ 54

1 We're a big family, and it's quite a small house. I share a bedroom with my two older brothers. My grandparents live with us too. It's cramped and noisy, but at least there's always someone around. It's the only house I've ever known. I love living with my family, we all get on so well. I suppose I'll move out when I get married. I don't know when that will be!

2 I had to move to London when I started work. I saw an advert in the paper for a room in a shared house. Well it's a flat on the first floor of a big house, actually. My flatmates are away working quite a lot, so it's just like living on my own a lot of the time, really … especially during the week. Weekends are different. I have to say that living with friends is more difficult than I thought it would be. For one thing, nobody ever wants to do any housework.

3 I'm in my last year at college and I'm really looking forward to finishing and going abroad or getting out of this town! I can't wait to get away from here and be independent. It's going to be brilliant. My sister and I have shared a room all our lives. My family's lovely, but I'd like to have the chance of my own space – preferably in a lovely sunny country somewhere.

▶ 56

1 As an architect, I'm interested in everything about house design. But we can learn so much from traditional buildings and designs. Traditional houses usually survive bad weather conditions better than modern ones, so the question is, what can we copy from those houses when we build new houses? Like the rock homes, you know? They heat up less quickly than brick houses, which is great in hot climates.

2 Well, a shelter is a lot less permanent and more basic than a house. The igloos that people build with ice in the Arctic region are a perfect example of a shelter. A shelter just protects you from the weather, but a home has several spaces with different uses.

3 I'd say a *ger* is both a shelter and a home. It's organized around a fire in the centre with a chimney, and it has separate areas for men and women. A *ger* isn't as solid as a brick or wooden house but you can take it down and put it up much faster, which is what nomadic people in Mongolia need.

4 Well, it all depends on the local weather. I mean, if you live in an area that has regular floods, it's a good idea to live in a house on stilts. That way, you can live much more safely above the water and you don't have to worry every time it rains a lot! And the higher the stilts, the safer you are!

5 I think that modern homes are fairly similar wherever they are in the world, which doesn't always mean that they are the best design for every situation. In our crowded cities, modern houses are getting smaller and smaller so that they can be built more cheaply. Unfortunately, sometimes modern houses are also built badly. They don't work as efficiently as traditional houses – they need central heating in winter and air conditioning in summer.

▶ 58

A = estate agent, C = customer

A: Good morning.

C: Hi, I'm interested in any properties you have in the town centre.

A: OK, and is that to rent or to buy?

C: Oh, it's to rent. I've just started a new job here, so I think I'd rather rent than buy, for now anyway.

A: Right, well we have quite a few flats on our system, from one-bed studios to four-bedroom apartments.

C: I'd prefer something small, but not too small. I imagine I'll get a lot of friends staying with me. So, two bedrooms, and preferably with a lift. I cycle a lot and I don't want to carry my bike up lots of stairs!

A: Well, most of the modern buildings have lifts, but a lot of the properties in the centre are quite old. Would you rather look at new places or older ones?

C: I don't mind, at this stage I'm just getting an idea of what things are like here.

A: OK … so you're new to the area?

C: Yeah, I lived in a little village up near the mountains until recently.

A: Oh, that sounds lovely.

C: To be honest, I prefer towns to villages. The problem with a village is that everyone knows your business. Maybe I'm unfriendly, but I like the way that in a town you don't know everyone.

A: Ah yes, I've heard a few people say that! To be honest, I prefer living here. I suppose I like my privacy too. Right, erm, what about garage space? Do you need that?

C: No, I haven't got a car, I prefer to walk or cycle. It keeps me fit.

A: Of course, you mentioned your bike!

C: Yeah! And anyway, in my experience, driving in town is a nightmare!

A: I know, and it's getting worse. OK, well, the next thing to consider is your budget and the rental period.

Unit 8

▶ 61

1 A couple of years ago I went on a round-the-world trip with a friend. What an experience! The best bits were when we took local buses and trains – you know the kind of thing. They stop everywhere and it takes ages to get to where you're going. On the other hand, we met some really interesting people on the buses in Peru. We learned a lot about the history of Peru. But I took far too much luggage with me – I couldn't carry it easily and I worried about losing it. Just take a small backpack with the essentials, that's my advice.

2 I haven't travelled very much in the last few years. I've been on a few day trips to Liverpool and I've had a couple of weekends away to Scotland this year. I don't go far any more. I'm more interested in the place I'm going to than in the journey. Edinburgh and Glasgow are fascinating cities. But in my experience, the key to a good trip is good planning. Don't leave anything to chance!

3 I work in IT and I travel a lot – too much – for my job. I spend a lot of time on planes and in my car on the motorway, travelling to the projects I'm working on. I don't particularly enjoy it, especially when there are delays, but it's part of my job. I often get a very early flight from Gatwick and delays can mean I lose a whole working day. I have to go on business trips abroad several times a year. My travel tip? Once the flight starts, take your watch off and relax. You have no control over the time you arrive, so why get stressed?

▶ 63

R = Rose, M = Matt

R: Hi there, I'm Rose.

M: Hi, I'm Matt.

R: Is this your first time in Corfu?

M: No, actually. We come every year. We love staying here.

R: So do we. We keep coming back year after year. It's hard to find somewhere with everything you need for a holiday – great beaches, fantastic weather and something for everyone to do.

M: I know. Actually, there's a paragliding class later – I fancy trying that.

R: My friends want to do that too! To be honest, lying by the pool is my idea of a holiday.

M: Oh, I get a bit bored with doing that after the first day or two. I need to move around and do things.

R: Well, why not? It's a different way of relaxing, I suppose.

M: Yes, that's right. Well, if you decide to go paragliding with your friends, we'll see you there!

▶ 65

When you've walked across half of Africa and you've walked up the west coast of North America, where do you go next? On tomorrow's show my guest is a man who can give us the answer. I'm talking about the conservationist Mike Fay – a man with a very personal way of saving what he calls the last wild places on Earth. For those of you who don't know Mike Fay, he does some unusual things in his work with the Wildlife Conservation Society. For instance, he's spent more than two years of his life trekking through some of the toughest places on the planet. And he often just takes a T-shirt, a pair of shorts and a pair of sandals on these treks. Fay says he has only slept in a bed about fifty times in ten years. The last time he was on the show, he'd just finished a survey of giant redwood trees on the west coast of the United States. What has he been doing since then? Well, he hasn't been taking it easy! In fact, recently he's been walking again, this time across Canada. In western Canada, mining companies have been looking for gold and oil. To do this, they've been digging up enormous areas – they've destroyed hundreds of square kilometres of wilderness. You can hear what Mike Fay feels about this in tomorrow's show. And we'll also find out what's been happening to national parks in Gabon since Fay was there. We know that people have been trying to set up mines near the parks and the Gabonese government has stopped at least two mining operations. Hear more tomorrow in my interview with Mike Fay, and find out what he thinks a population of seven billion people might do to our planet.

▶ 67

T = tourist, G = guide

1

T: I wonder if you could help us. Our luggage hasn't arrived.

G: Right. Are you with SunnyTimes tours?

T: Yes. Mr and Mrs Cameron.

G: And which flight were you on, Mrs Cameron?

T: The FastJet flight from Manchester. I think it's FJ2498. We've been talking to some of the other passengers and their luggage has come through, no problem.

G: Ah, yes. It seems some bags have gone to another airport. Flight FJ2498?

T: Yes, that's right. Do you know which airport our bags have gone to?

G: Yes, I'm afraid the luggage has gone to Rome.

T: Rome? How did that happen?

G: I'm not sure, but all the missing bags are coming on the next flight.

T: But when's the next flight?

G: It's tomorrow morning. Don't worry, we'll arrange everything. Which hotel are you staying at? Your bags will go there directly.

T: But all our summer clothes are in the suitcases.

2

G: Hello, Mr Jones. Is anything wrong? Can I help?

T: Well, it's about my wife, actually. She hasn't been feeling well for a couple of days.

G: I'm sorry to hear that. Is it something she's eaten, do you think? Or just travel sickness?

T: I don't know. She's had a temperature all night, but she feels cold.

G: OK, … erm, how long has she been feeling like this?

T: A couple of days? Yes, since the boat trip on Tuesday. Is there anything you can do?

G: Well it's probably nothing to worry about. But I'll ask the hotel to arrange for a doctor, just in case.

T: That's great, thank you.

Unit 9

▶ 70

R = researcher, S = shopper

1

R: Hi, do you mind if I ask you some quick questions about your shopping today?

S: Not at all, no.

R: Lovely. Well, first, can I ask what you've bought?

S: Oh yes, I've bought the latest iPhone.

R: Is it for you?

S: No, for my mum. For Mother's Day, next Sunday. She's really into gadgets and technology.

2

R: Hello, you look happy. Have you bought something nice?

S: Erm, I've got a couple of nice shirts in the sale, actually. That's all I came in for.

R: And who did you buy them for?

S: Just for myself. I buy all my clothes in the sales.

R: OK!

3

R: Hi, have you got time to answer a quick question or two?

S: Yes, I think so. We need a break!

R: Have you been spending a lot of money?

S: No, that's the problem! We're looking for some nice jewellery, earrings or a gold chain maybe … but we can't find anything we like.

R: And who is it for?

S: It's just for ourselves. We usually buy each other something special for our anniversary every year. It's a little tradition we have.

R: Well, good luck!

▶ 73

D = Dan, S = Samira

D: So, Samira, have you read any interesting articles this week?

S: Yes, I have, Dan. Several websites have articles about impulse buying. They're based on a study by the BBC.

D: And impulse buying is … ?

S: OK, have you ever gone to the shops to buy just one or two items – like bread and milk – and come back with loads of things you hadn't intended to buy? Well, that's impulse buying. Buying things just because you see them, without really thinking about it.

D: Oh, that sounds like me.

S: Well, don't worry, you're not alone. We've probably all done it at one time or other. And in fact, the study says that about five per cent of us have even spent more than £500 on a purchase that wasn't necessary!

D: But sometimes you see special offers or good deals on things. Especially on electrical goods like TVs or tablets. If we can save a bit of money, that's good isn't it?

S: OK, but as it says in a couple of the articles, the fact that something is good value for money doesn't matter if you can't afford it! You should always have a budget – work out how much you can spend and then stick to that amount. Anyway, there are some points in the research I thought were really interesting. The study divided people into two groups – men and women.
If you're female and under twenty-one, you're more likely to buy on impulse. Apparently, many women, but few men, use shopping as a way of managing their mood when they're unhappy. Also, if you go shopping when you're hungry, you're more likely to buy loads of food.

D: Oh, that explains why I spend too much money at the supermarket! So I just need to make sure I have a snack before I go?

S: Yes, that and make a list. Actually, there are plenty of simple things you can do to avoid impulse buying. You just need to take a little time to plan your shopping and you'll save money.

▶ 77

A = assistant, C = customer

1

A: Can I help you at all?

C: Yes, can I have a look at this silver chain?

A: This one?

C: Yes, please.

A: It's lovely, isn't it? Is it for you?

C: No, for my sister.

A: It's in the sale actually – it's got twenty per cent off.

C: Oh? I like it, but it's a bit heavy. I was looking for something lighter.

A: How about this?

C: Yeah, that's great. That's just right, I think. Erm, can she return it if she doesn't like it, though?

A: Yes, she can exchange it within ten days.

C: OK, good.

A: That's as long as she's got the receipt, of course.

C: I'll take it then. Can you gift-wrap it for me?

A: Well we don't actually do gift-wrapping, but we have some nice gift boxes for sale, over there.

C: Right.

2

C: Excuse me, are you in this department?

A: Yes, can I help you?

C: Well, I'm looking for a sofa that I saw on your website, but I can't see it here.

A: OK, do you have the reference number or the model name?

C: Yes, it's Byunk. The number is 00 389 276.

A: Right, let me see if it's in stock.

C: The website said 'available' this morning …

A: Yes, here we are. Do you want it in red, grey or blue?

C: Blue, if you've got it.

A: Yes, there are plenty in stock. Just give them this reference number at the collection point.

C: OK. What about delivery? How much do you charge for delivery?

A: Can you tell me your postcode? The charges go by area.

C: NE4 6AP

A: That would be £55.

C: Wow… OK.

A: If you go to the customer service desk, they can take your details and arrange the delivery date.

C: And do I pay here or … ?

A: The tills are by the collection point. You can pay by card or in cash.

C: Right, thanks for your help. Erm, how do I get to the tills, sorry?

A: Just follow the yellow arrows.

Unit 10

▶ 80

This man is Steve Holman. He's 52 years old and his friends think he's crazy. Why? Because he's running 200 kilometres in the Sahara desert. And he has to carry all his food with him, in a backpack that weighs twelve kilos. With the temperature hitting 38 degrees, he struggles up enormous sand dunes, sometimes crawling on his hands and knees. This is the annual *Marathon des Sables*, one of the key events on the ultrarunning calendar. Any race longer than a regular 42-kilometre marathon is called ultrarunning, but there is more to this kind of running than simply the distance. Ultrarunners push the human body to incredible limits and learn that it's stronger than you'd imagine. Another ultrarunner is Leslie Antonis, who ran 160 kilometres in 34 hours at the age of 47. It's amazing what the human body can do!

▶ 82

P = Peter, G = Gail

P: Now I'm sure most of us are amazed when we watch the Paralympics and we see athletes who run a marathon on blades or play rugby in a wheelchair. Tonight on Channel 10, there's a documentary which features some famous Paralympians. Gail, you've seen a preview of the programme.

G: Yes, Peter. The programme is a fascinating look at how medical science is changing people's lives right now. The Paralympians you mentioned use blades and wheelchairs, but these are devices that don't actually give them extra power. We also see some athletes whose devices are bionic.

P: And what's the difference, exactly?

G: I suppose the simplest explanation of a bionic device is one that uses electronics in some way. Sometimes they have their own power. And in sports, this means you can improve your performance.

P: So you mean bionic hands or arms?

G: Yes, and bionic legs too. Now there are also wheelchairs which are controlled electronically by the user.

P: So bionics is great news for patients who have lost the use of a limb.

G: Absolutely. And the range of bionic devices the programme describes is growing all the time. Let me tell you about a woman whose life suddenly changed after a skiing accident. Her name's Amanda Boxtel – she lost the use of her legs and didn't walk for over twenty years. Now she can use a robotic structure which supports her body so that she can walk. The structure she uses is called an exo-skeleton. Amanda used to be an athlete, but these days she works with an organization that promotes bionic technology.

P: And I believe there are already devices that help blind people to see and deaf people to hear.

G: That's right. It seems as if there's no limit to the things bionic devices will be able to do. So don't forget to watch the programme on Channel 10 tonight at 9.30.

▶ 86

1

A: What on earth has happened to you? There's blood all down your leg!

B: Oh, it's nothing. I tripped up when I was out running. I fell on a bit of tree or something.

A: Let me see. Oh, that looks nasty! It's quite a deep cut. You'd better wash it straightaway.

B: Yeah, I will.

A: You know, if I were you, I'd go down to A and E. I'd get it looked at.

B: It doesn't hurt. It's just a cut, really. I'm not going all the way to the hospital about a cut on my leg.

A: Hmm, it might need stitches, though. I would keep an eye on it if I were you.

B: OK, if it doesn't stop bleeding, I'll give the surgery a ring and see if the nurse is there.

A: Good, because I don't think we've got any plasters big enough!

2

C: Is my neck red? I think I've been stung or something.

D: A bit, yeah. It looks a bit swollen. Is it itchy?

C: Not exactly. It's painful rather than really itchy. How funny, I don't usually react to insect bites and stuff. Oooh, I feel a bit sick, actually.

D: You should put some antihistamine cream on it and see if it gets better.

C: Have you got any?

D: Yes, I'm sure I've got some somewhere. You'll have to check the date on the tube, though. I'm not sure how long I've had it.

3

E: Ow!

F: Is your wrist still hurting you?

E: Yeah, actually it is. It hurts when I move it.

F: It might be worth getting it X-rayed. It's been, what, three days now? I wouldn't just ignore it, you might have broken something.

E: No, you're probably right. But I'm sure it's just a sprain, from when I fell against the table …

F: Even so, it's probably best to get it looked at.

E: Hmm.

F: Why don't you go and see Rosana in reception? She's the first-aid person. She'll know.

E: Good idea.

Unit 11

▶ 88

I = interviewer

1

I: Do you follow the news?

M: Yes, most of the time. I get the headlines direct to my mobile so that I can keep up with business news. I never buy a paper. I just catch up with the news online. Every couple of days, I have a quick look through the world news or at the comment and analysis sections, and I bookmark an article if it looks interesting.

2

I: How often do you read or buy a newspaper?

W: Oh! I don't read the papers, I haven't got time. I can see the news on my tablet, but I don't usually click on headlines unless they're about celebrities. If there's a video clip, then I might have a quick look at that. I prefer that to reading.

3

I: What kind of news stories interest you?

M: I like stories about my town, so I follow a couple of local websites. Also, celebrity interviews are always fun to read, but I don't believe everything I read because journalists sometimes change people's words. But I usually read the gossip column when I'm on the bus rather than the serious news.

4

I: How often do you share news stories you see online?

W: I sometimes send a story to friends if it's something that makes me laugh. I wouldn't share the big headline stories because they're probably reading about them anyway. I mean, we've got 24-hour news on TV and live streams of news online all day, haven't we?

▶ 90

1

A: I like this Twitter travel idea.

B: What's that?

A: It's this travel journalist, Rita Shaw. She goes off to different places and asks her followers on social media to suggest things to do. You know, 'I've just got off the train in Paris and I'm feeling hungry. Where can I get a good breakfast?' That sort of thing.

B: OK. And then what happens?

A: And then she writes about it. It's like a travel guide by the people who live in places – they're the ones who really know what's good. It's a great idea to use social media for something like that.

B: I didn't realize social media could actually be useful for anything!

2

C: It says here there's an eclipse tomorrow. Did you know?

D: Tomorrow? I thought it was today.

C: No, tomorrow. We should be able to see it from here. I'm just looking at this weather website. It's reminding people not to look at it with telescopes.

D: Yeah, I know.

C: It's quite a good website, actually. It tells you all sorts of things.

D: I know. I've got it bookmarked.

C: Oh, I wondered if you had.

3

E: Wow, that's terrible. Have you seen this? It's bad enough to lose your job, but finding out from a text!

F: I saw that story. The company sent about 200 employees a text message. They told them not to turn up for work on Monday.

E: I didn't think that you could do that.

F: Me neither, but there you go …

4

G: Oh, that's hilarious!

H: Hmm … ?

G: You know that weird politician, the one who believes in UFOs?

H: Oh yeah, I can't remember his name, but I know who you mean.

G: He's posted a video on the internet. He's invited 'all friendly aliens' to come to a meeting in the Houses of Parliament.

H: No way! I didn't know you followed him online.

G: I don't, but there's an article about it in the paper. Look!

▶ 92

1 a: How much did the coffee cost?

 b: What? You asked me to get tea.

2 c: We need to send a text about this.

 d: What? I thought you said send an email.

3 e: I'm going home now.

 f: Really? You said you were staying.

4 g: I heard that story on the news yesterday.

 h: Really? It wasn't in the papers.

▶ 94

1

A = answerphone, R = Roger

A: The person you are calling is not available. Please leave a message after the tone.

R: Hi, this is a message for Anna Price. It's about the apartment for rent in the town centre, the one advertised in the Town Hall. OK, er, my name is Roger, I'm on 96235601. So, I'll try and call you later if I don't hear from you first. Thanks.

2

R = Roger, S = secretary

S: P and Q Associates, good morning.

R: Oh, hello. Could I speak to Jess Parker, please?

S: I'm afraid she's not in the office at the moment. Can I take a message?

R: Actually I'm returning her call. She left me a message this morning.

S: OK, I'll let her know that you rang. Who's calling?

R: It's Roger Lee. She has my number.

S: OK well, I'm sure she'll get back to you as soon as she comes in, Mr Lee.

R: Right, thanks.

▶ 95

1

T = Tony, A = Anna

T: Morning, Anna!

A: Oh, hi Tony. Oh, someone called about the apartments in the town centre. He called my number, but it should go to you really. You're handling those apartments, aren't you? Let me see, his name's Roger and his number is 96235601, but he said he'd call back.

T: OK, thanks. I'll give him a ring.

2

J = Jess, S = secretary

J: Hi, I'm back.

S: Hi, Jess. Just a moment, there were a couple of calls for you while you were out. Suzy … she said she would call back … and a guy called Roger said he was returning your call.

J: OK, thanks. Any more?

S: No, that's all.

▶ **96**

1 Could I speak to Jess Parker, please?

2 Can you give her a message?

3 I wonder whether I could leave a message?

4 I wonder if you could tell her I called?

Unit 12

▶ **97**

I = interviewer, F = farmer

I: I'm here on the Isle of Lewis, in the Hebrides. It takes almost three hours to get here on the ferry from the Scottish mainland, so obviously it's not a journey people do every day. The traditional industries in the Hebrides include farming sheep and fishing. I'm with Alistair, a Hebridean farmer. Alistair, you were telling me about moving sheep by boat. That sounds like a difficult task! I've never heard of putting sheep in a boat before.

F: Well, it's not as hard as it sounds. It's normal practice for us.

I: Why do you need to move the sheep like this? Where do you take them?

F: We move them over to a small island for the summer, where there's plenty of grass for them to eat. The thing is, we can only fit a few in the boat, so we have to go back and forward a few times.

I: And when do you bring them back?

F: We normally go and get them to bring them back to the main island for the winter. We fetch them before the bad weather starts, usually in September. So, do you want to come across to the island with me one day?

I: OK! Why not? It should be interesting.

▶ **99**

E = Emma, B = Beth

(The words of Emma Stokes are spoken by an actor.)

E: The first real eye-opener I had of what life was like in the African forest was on my first-ever expedition. It was the first day and we ended up making camp early that evening. I was exhausted and I fell fast asleep straightaway.

About four hours later, I was woken up by a lot of screaming and shouting and the words NJOKO, NJOKO! It was the local trackers shouting. Then I heard loud trumpeting and sounds of heavy steps. Basically, we'd put our tent in the middle of a giant elephant path. We couldn't have picked a more inappropriate place! By the time I'd managed to get all my gear and get out of the tent, all of the trackers and all of the local guides had already disappeared into the night. When we came back, three of the tents were completely destroyed. That was my first taste of where not to set up a camp in the forest.

(The words of Beth Shapiro are spoken by an actor.)

B: A couple of summers ago we went to Siberia. We were looking for mammoth bones and tusks, and even hoping to find some mammoth mummies. We flew in on a small plane. It's pretty remote and there are no people there. When you land and get out of the plane, you look around and there's nothing there. And you set up your camp and there's still nothing there. And you're sitting there, relaxing, in total silence and there's nothing … Then all of a sudden, you're joined by ten million mosquitoes. I remember we made this kind of rice and fish dish for dinner, and we were sitting there, trying to enjoy this rice and fish meal … being eaten alive by mosquitoes. We had nets over our heads, but they were totally inadequate. The mosquitoes could still bite you. And you had to take the net off in order to eat. Every time you did that, hundreds of mosquitoes landed all over your face. They got in the food as well. It was just one part rice, one part fish and one part mosquito! You could go mad after just a few days of that!

▶ **102**

1

A: Is everything OK with your food?

B: Yes, yes, it's lovely. But, erm, I should have told you that I don't eat meat.

A: Oh! Oh dear!

B: I'm really sorry you've gone to all this trouble.

A: There's no need to apologize – it's not a problem.

B: No, I should have said something earlier.

A: It's OK. I should have asked you if there was anything you couldn't eat. It's my fault. I'll make you something else.

B: No, please don't. The vegetables are delicious and there's plenty to eat.

A: Are you sure?

B: Yes, really. I'm enjoying this. I'll just leave the meat if that's OK with you.

A: OK.

2

C: Oh, my goodness! What was that?

D: I dropped the tray of glasses!

C: Oh, those nice glasses from Italy …

D: I couldn't help it – I slipped.

C: Are you OK? Let me help you up. You are clumsy, though.

D: Don't blame me – this floor is slippery.

C: Yes, but if you'd been more careful …

D: Look, it was an accident! It could have happened to anyone.

C: I know, I know. It's not your fault. Sorry I got upset.

D: It is a shame about those glasses, though. We've only just got them!

3

E: I'm so sorry to keep you waiting. The bus didn't come!

F: Were you waiting for the number 46?

E: Yes, it was supposed to come at half past five.

F: Don't worry about it – that service is terrible. It's always late.

E: I tried to phone you, but I couldn't get through.

F: Ah, I think my phone is switched off! Sorry about that!

E: Goodness, I'm almost an hour late!

F: It's OK. It's just one of those things – buses are unreliable! Anyway, you're here now and that's the main thing.

NATIONAL GEOGRAPHIC
LEARNING

Life Intermediate Student's Book Split B,
2nd Edition
Helen Stephenson, Paul Dummett, John Hughes

Vice President, Editorial Director:
  John McHugh

Executive Editor: Sian Mavor

Publishing Consultant: Karen Spiller

Project Manager: Laura Brant

Development Editor: Liz Driscoll

Editorial Manager: Claire Merchant

Head of Strategic Marketing ELT:
  Charlotte Ellis

Senior Content Project Manager:
  Nick Ventullo

Manufacturing Manager: Eyvett Davis

Senior IP Analyst: Ashley Maynard

Senior IP Project Manager:
  Michelle McKenna

Cover: Lisa Trager

Text design: emc design ltd.

Compositor: emc design ltd.

Audio: Tom Dick and Debbie Productions Ltd

Contributing Writer: Graham Burton
  (Grammar summary)

For product information and technology assistance, contact us at
Cengage Learning Customer & Sales Support, cengage.com/contact
For permission to use material from this text or product,
submit all requests online at **cengage.com/permissions**
Further permissions questions can be emailed to
permissionrequest@cengage.com

ISBN: 978-1-337-63148-8

National Geographic Learning
Cheriton House, North Way,
Andover, Hampshire, SP10 5BE
United Kingdom

National Geographic Learning, a Cengage Learning Company, has a mission to bring the world to the classroom and the classroom to life. With our English language programs, students learn about their world by experiencing it. Through our partnerships with National Geographic and TED Talks, they develop the language and skills they need to be successful global citizens and leaders.

Locate your local office at **international.cengage.com/region**

Visit National Geographic Learning online at **NGL.Cengage.com/ELT**
Visit our corporate website at **www.cengage.com**

CREDITS
Text: p10: source: 'Before New York', by Peter Miller, National Geographic. http://ngm.nationalgeographic.com/2009/09/manhattan/miller-text; p15: source: 'Sweet songs and strong coffee', by Àitor Garrido Jiménez, allgristthemill.blogspot.co.uk; p22: source: 'Holidays and memories', NG Traveler, National Geographic, April 2013; p24: sources: 'Walking for wildlife', by Mike Fay, National Geographic. http://www.nationalgeographic.com/explorers/bios/michael-fay/, http://kids.nationalgeographic.com/explore/explorers/interview-with-mike-fay/ and http://radio.nationalgeographic.com/radio/ng-weekend-archives/1205/; p39: source: 'The art of the deal', by Andrew McCarthy, National Geographic, January/February 2011, http://travel.nationalgeographic.com/travel/countries/morocco-traveler/; p51: source: 'Diane Van Deren', by Andrea Minarcek, National Geographic, 2009. http://adventure.nationalgeographic.com/, and source: 'John Bul Dau, Humanitarian', National Geographic. www.nationalgeographic.com/; p70: source: 'Want to search for the Northwest Passage like a 19th-century British explorer? Bring your sterling silverware and hubris', by Mary Anne Potts, National Geographic, April 07, 2010. ngadventure.typepad.com/blog/2010/04/want-to-seach-for-the-northwest-passage-like-a-19thcentury-british-explorer-bring-your-sterling-silv.html; p72: source: 'Experts in the wild', by Emma Stokes, National Geographic. http://www.nationalgeographic.com/field/explorers/emma-stokes/, and source 'Experts in the wild', by Beth Shapiro, National Geographic. http://www.nationalgeographic.com/field/explorers/beth-shapiro/; p75: source: 'The Samurai Way', by Tom O'Neill, National Geographic, December 2003, p. 98.
Cover: © Atlantide Phototravel/Getty Images.
Photos: 6 (t) Andrew Wilson/Alamy Stock Photo; 6 (m) © TebNad/Shutterstock.com; 6 (bl) © NurPhoto/Getty Images; 6 (br) © Cory Richards/National Geographic Creative; 7 (tl) © NASA; 7 (tr) © Krystle Wright/National Geographic Creative; 7 (bl) © Aaron Huey/National Geographic Creative; 7 (br) © Chris Caldicott/Design Pics/Getty Images; 8 (tl) © Erika Larsen/National Geographic Creative; 8 (tm) © Austin Beahm; 8 (tr) © Kos Picture Source/Getty Images; 8 (mtl) © Charles Stinson Photography; 8 (mtm) © Brian Finke c/o Everybody Somebody Inc/National Geographic Creative; 8 (mtr) © Andrew Lever/4Corners Image Library;

Printed in China by RR Donnelley
Print Number: 01 Print Year: 2018

8 (mbl) © Brian Skerry/National Geographic Creative; 8 (mbm) © Jonathan & Angela Scott/AWL Images/Getty Images; 8 (mbr) © Arcansel/Shutterstock.com; 8 (bl) © Pierre Verdy /AFP/Getty Images; 8 (bm) © Chris Rainier; 8 (br) © Jim Richardson/National Geographic Creative; 9 © Brian Skerry/National Geographic Creative; 10–11 (t) © Markley Boyer/National Geographic Creative; 10–11 (b) © Robert Clark/National Geographic Creative; 12 (tl) © Apurva Madia/Shutterstock.com; 12 (tr) © David Edwards/National Geographic Creative; 12 (bl) © Claudiovidri/Shutterstock.com; 12 (br) © Frans Lanting/National Geographic Creative; 15 (all) © Amy Toensing/National Geographic Creative; 16 Image Source/Alamy Stock Photo; 18 © TebNad/Shutterstock.com; 20 © Donald Miralle/ Getty Images; 21 © Jonathan & Angela Scott/AWL Images/Getty Images; 22 © Sean Gallagher/National Geographic Creative; 24 © Michael Nichols/National Geographic Creative; 27 © Fabi Fliervoet; 28 © koh sze kiat/Shutterstock.com; 29 © William Perugini/ Shutterstock.com; 30 © Cory Richards/National Geographic Creative; 32 © Pius Lee/Shutterstock.com; 33 © Arcansel/Shutterstock. com; 34 (t) keith morris/Alamy Stock Photo; 34 (b) © Chris Ratcliffe/Bloomberg/Getty Images; 35 © Mariana Greif Etchebehere/ Bloomberg/Getty Images; 36 © Matt McClain/The Washington Post/Getty Images; 37 Roger Davies/Alamy Stock Photo; 38 © Chris Rainier/National Geographic Creative; 39 © Angiolo Manetti: 40 © pcruciatti/Shutterstock.com; 41 (t) LAMB/Alamy Stock Photo; 41 (b) © topnatthapon/Shutterstock.com; 42 © Jonathan Knowles/Getty Images; 44 (tl) © withGod/Shutterstock.com; 44 (tr) © Sylvie Bouchard/Shutterstock.com; 44 (bl) © Salvador Aznar/Shutterstock.com; 44 (br) © Peter Wollinga/Shutterstock.com; 45 © Pierre Verdy /AFP/Getty Images; 46 titoOnz/Alamy Stock Photo; 48 © Michael Buholzer/AFP/Getty Images; 49 © Bryan Christie Design; 51 (t) © Masterfile Royalty Free; 51 (b) © Mark Thiessen/National Geographic Creative; 52 mark phillips/Alamy Stock Photo; 53 © Martin Valigursky/Shutterstock.com; 54 (inset) ITAR-TASS Photo Agency/Alamy Stock Photo; 54 © NASA; 56 © Jimmy Chin and Lynsey Dyer/ National Geographic Creative; 57 © Chris Rainier; 58 © Ricardo Stuckert; 59 © Michael Nichols/National Geographic Creative; 60 © STRDEL/Stringer/Getty Images; 63 © Matthieu Paley/National Geographic Creative; 64 © Dragon Images/Shutterstock.com; 66 © NurPhoto/Getty Images; 67 Illustration by www.british-sign.co.uk; 68 Arina Habich/Alamy Stock Photo; 69 © Jim Richardson/National Geographic Creative; 70 © 2011 by Anchor Books, a division of Penguin Random House Group Inc., from "The Man Who Ate His Boots: The Tragic History of the Search for the Northeast Passage" by Anthony Brandt. Used by permission of Alfred A. Knopf, a division of Random House Inc.; 70–71 © Paul Nicklen/National Geographic Creative; 72 (t) © John Goodrich/National Geographic Creative; 72 (b) © Beth Shapiro/National Geographic Creative; 73 © Lynn Johnson/National Geographic Creative; 75 © Ira Block/National Geographic Creative; 76 © Birgid Allig/Getty Images; 77 © Image Source/Getty Images; 78 Danita Delimont/Alamy Stock Photo; 80 © Steve Winter/ National Geographic Creative.

ACKNOWLEDGEMENTS

The *Life* publishing team would like to thank the following teachers and students who provided invaluable and detailed feedback on the first edition:

Armik Adamians, Colombo Americano, Cali; Carlos Alberto Aguirre, Universidad Madero, Puebla; Anabel Aikin, La Escuela Oficial de Idiomas de Coslada, Madrid; Pamela Alvarez, Colegio Eccleston, Lanús; Manuel Antonio, CEL – Unicamp, São Paolo; Bob Ashcroft, Shonan Koka University; Linda Azzopardi, Clubclass; Éricka Bauchwitz, Universidad Madero, Puebla; Paola Biancolini, Università Cattolica del Sacro Cuore, Milan; Laura Bottiglieri, Universidad Nacional de Salta; Richard Brookes, Brookes Talen, Aalsmeer; Maria Cante, Universidad Madero, Puebla; Carmín Castillo, Universidad Madero, Puebla; Ana Laura Chacón, Universidad Madero, Puebla; Somchao Chatnaridom, Suratthani Rajabhat University, Surat Thani; Adrian Cini, British Study Centres, London; Andrew Clarke, Centre of English Studies, Dublin; Mariano Cordoni, Centro Universitario de Idiomas, Buenos Aires; Monica Cuellar, Universidad La Gran Colombia; Jacqui Davis-Bowen, St Giles International; Nuria Mendoza Dominguez, Universidad Nebrija, Madrid; Robin Duncan, ITC London; Christine Eade, Libera Università Internazionale degli Studi Sociali Guido Carli, Rome; Leopoldo Pinzon Escobar, Universidad Catolica; Joanne Evans, Linguarama, Berlin; Juan David Figueroa, Colombo Americano, Cali; Emmanuel Flores, Universidad del Valle de Puebla; Sally Fryer, University of Sheffield, Sheffield; Antonio David Berbel García, Escuela Oficial de Idiomas de Almería; Lia Gargioni, Feltrinelli Secondary School, Milan; Roberta Giugni, Galileo Galilei Secondary School, Legnano; Monica Gomez, Universidad Pontificia Bolivariana; Doctor Erwin Gonzales, Centro de Idiomas Universidad Nacional San Agustin; Ivonne Gonzalez, Universidad de La Sabana; J Gouman, Pieter Zandt Scholengemeenschap, Kampen; Cherryll Harrison, UNINT, Rome; Lottie Harrison, International House Recoleta; Marjo Heij, CSG Prins Maurits, Middelharnis; María del Pilar Hernández, Universidad Madero, Puebla; Luz Stella Hernandez, Universidad de La Sabana; Rogelio Herrera, Colombo Americano, Cali; Amy Huang, Language Canada, Taipei; Huang Huei-Jiun, Pu Tai Senior High School; Nelson Jaramillo, Colombo Americano, Cali; Jacek Kaczmarek, Xiehe YouDe High School, Taipei; Thurgadevi Kalay, Kaplan; Noreen Kane, Centre of English Studies, Dublin; Billy Kao, Jinwen University of Science and Technology; Shih-Fan Kao, Jinwen University of Science and Technology, Taipei; Youmay Kao, Mackay Junior College of Medicine, Nursing, and Management, Taipei; Fleur Kelder, Vechtstede College, Weesp; Dr Sarinya Khattiya, Chiang Mai University; Lucy Khoo, Kaplan; Karen Koh, Kaplan; Susan Langerfeld, Liceo Scientifico Statale Augusto Righi, Rome; Hilary Lawler, Centre of English Studies, Dublin; Eva Lendi, Kantonsschule Zürich Nord, Zürich; Evon Lo, Jinwen University of Science and Technology; Peter Loftus, Centre of English Studies, Dublin; José Luiz, Inglês com Tecnologia, Cruzeiro; Christopher MacGuire, UC Language Center; Eric Maher, Centre of English Studies, Dublin; Nick Malewski, ITC London; Claudia Maribell Loo, Universidad Madero, Puebla; Malcolm Marr, ITC London; Graciela Martin, ICANA (Belgrano); Erik Meek, CS Vincent van Gogh, Assen; Marlene Merkt, Kantonsschule Zürich Nord, Zürich; David Moran, Qatar University, Doha; Rosella Morini, Feltrinelli Secondary School, Milan; Judith Mundell, Quarenghi Adult Learning Centre, Milan; Cinthya Nestor, Universidad Madero, Puebla; Peter O'Connor, Musashino University, Tokyo; Cliona O'Neill, Trinity School, Rome; María José Colón Orellana, Escola Oficial d'Idiomes de Terrassa, Barcelona; Viviana Ortega, Universidad Mayor, Santiago; Luc Peeters, Kyoto Sangyo University, Kyoto; Sanja Brekalo Pelin, La Escuela Oficial de Idiomas de Coslada, Madrid; Itzel Carolina Pérez, Universidad Madero, Puebla; Sutthima Peung, Rajamangala University of Technology Rattanakosin; Marina Pezzuoli, Liceo Scientifico Amedeo Avogadro, Rome; Andrew Pharis, Aichi Gakuin University, Nagoya; Hugh Podmore, St Giles International; Carolina Porras, Universidad de La Sabana; Brigit Portilla, Colombo Americano, Cali; Soudaben Pradeep, Kaplan; Judith Puertas, Colombo Americano, Cali; Takako Ramsden, Kyoto Sangyo University, Kyoto; Sophie Rebel-Dijkstra, Aeres Hogeschool; Zita Reszler, Nottingham Language Academy, Nottingham; Sophia Rizzo, St Giles International; Gloria Stella Quintero Riveros, Universidad Catolica; Cecilia Rosas, Euroidiomas; Eleonora Salas, IICANA Centro, Córdoba; Victoria Samaniego, La Escuela Oficial de Idiomas de Pozuelo de Alarcón, Madrid; Jeanette Sandre, Universidad Madero, Puebla; Bruno Scafati, ARICANA; Anya Shaw, International House Belgrano; Anne Smith, UNINT, Rome & University of Rome Tor Vergata; Suzannah Spencer-George, British Study Centres, Bournemouth; Students of Cultura Inglesa, São Paolo; Makiko Takeda, Aichi Gakuin University, Nagoya; Jilly Taylor, British Study Centres, London; Juliana Trisno, Kaplan; Ruey Miin Tsao, National Cheng Kung University, Tainan City; Michelle Uitterhoeve, Vechtstede College, Weesp; Anna Maria Usai, Liceo Spallanzani, Rome; Carolina Valdiri, Colombo Americano, Cali; Gina Vasquez, Colombo Americano, Cali; Andreas Vikran, NET School of English, Milan; Helen Ward, Oxford; Mimi Watts, Università Cattolica del Sacro Cuore, Milan; Yvonne Wee, Kaplan Higher Education Academy; Christopher Wood, Meijo University; Yanina Zagarrio, ARICANA.